THE WOMAN AND THE WAR BABY

OTHER BOOKS BY BILL RANSOM

Finding True North & Critter

Waving Arms at the Blind

The Single Man Looks at Winter

Last Call

Last Rites

Semaphore

The Jesus Incident (with Frank Herbert)

The Lazarus Effect (with Frank Herbert)

The Ascension Factor (with Frank Herbert)

Vira Vax

Burn

Learning the Ropes

Sleight of Hand

for Mary, with admiration
for your work and appreciation
for your company and conversation
—Bill

THE WOMAN AND THE WAR BABY

Poetry by

Bill Ransom (signature)

Bill Ransom

Jackson Hole 2014

BLUE BEGONIA PRESS § YAKIMA, WASHINGTON

billransom@hotmail.com

ACKNOWLEDGMENTS

Certain of these works have appeared in the following publications, with the author's gratitude to the editors:

Puerto del Sol, Waving Arms at the Blind, Finding True North, Bestiary, Another Kind of Nation: Contemporary Chinese Poetry, So Translating Rivers and Cities, Oregon Literary Review, Semaphore, Brooding Heron Press, *Silver Vain, The Single Man Looks at Winter, Slackwater Review, Willow Springs Magazine, Chariton Review, Pacific Search Magazine, Last Call, New York Quarterly, Tendril, War Baby* (CD).

Thanks to Ken Brewer, at whose urging I began this project; to Sam Green and Primus St. John for their encouragement to complete it; and to Jim and Karen Bodeen for having the faith and courage to present it to the world.

Muchas gracias, también a Carolina, Margarita, Beatríz, Cristina y Adriana para su amistad y las oportunidades de trabajar en Centroamérica.

ISBN: 978-0-911287-62-2
ISBN: 0-911287-62-0

Library of Congress Cataloging-in-Publication Data

Ransom, Bill.
  The woman and the war baby : poetry / by Bill Ransom.
    p. cm.
  ISBN 978-0-911287-62-2 (pbk. : alk. paper)
  I. Title.
  PS3568.A577W66 2008
  811'.54--dc22
  2008037143

Creation of this work was made possible in part by a National Endowment for the Arts fellowship, by a Centrum residency and by an Artist Trust Grants for Artist Projects (GAP) award.

Blue Begonia Press
225 South 15th Avenue
Yakima, WA 98902
Bluebegoniapress.com

THE WOMAN AND THE WAR BABY

CONTENTS

A moment of silence for the women and the war babies.

Orientation 1.

You'll know if you're made for this
when you bag your first body part.

WATER

Here lies one whose name was writ in water.
—John Keats

We breathe water first, gift of stardust and lightning.
Head down, afloat in Mom, we suck wet fists, cry, drool,
sweat and pee. Snot. Our small ocean rocks to the tide
of mother's life; our own tiny sea, squeezed in its four chambered fist,
squirts upon the shores of brain, pancreas, spleen and lung—lung
micropocked with those little alveoli, each a tiny gill
clutching its single drop of holy water that hands off oxygen to iron.
Motherwater births us all.
Washed in tears, our precious globes of water and light
translate ice crystals circling the moon
rainbows, fog, waterfalls, wavetops flashing sunset,
swamps and lakes and rain. And one silver drop
dangling at the tip of a lover's nose on a crisp winter morning,
frost on a buddy's beard, hot woodcutter breath against the chill.
Sap.

The woman who plays imaginary piano for her potato...

spends her days cooking potatoes and fish for a British archeologist at Luxor. At night, the archeologist drinks wine and plays a Yamaha keyboard for his friends, while the woman sits in her nearby room and unrolls across her lap a shawl that she has knitted up with the forbidden image of the black-and-white keys. She feels the counterpoint strong in her thighs, where her fingers tap out patterns of love, and she sees herself playing for the All-Knowing One on a black-lacquered piano in a great hall of stone and blue tile. Her potato with the single sprout balances in a white demitasse that she bought one cacophonous afternoon in Cairo. She pinned to her potato a magazine photo of the baldheaded archeologist and tonight, long after his keyboard stops, she patters out the syncopation of her dreams, her spirit and her complicated heart.

squats at the tiller of her boat, steers with her left armpit and plays her life out on a well-carved transom. Both legs blew into mist on a paddy-dike when she was twelve, so she keeps her blunt fingers twice busy. A red-haired medic gave her mother medicines, dressings, a bag of potatoes, but no word of her father. Now she sells potatoes from her boat, far downriver, while searching for word of her father. Her seed potato crouches atop its damp dishrag in the bow, scouting for snags while she plays the old French waltzes her mother loves and her grandmother hates so much. Her French grandfather died at Dien Ben Phu for stubbornness and for stupidity, her grandmother says. Her mother married a black-skinned man whom the Kennedy sent to vaccinate her village. They killed the Kennedy a few months later and her father left them for the Montagnards. He spoke a kind of French from the south of America, so she plays the French waltzes for him now, fingers oiling the mahogany transom, plays her music hard downriver and across the unforgiving sea. He will waltz back on the wind to her mother, who took no other man. Her seed potato nods with the chop of the river, or with the rhythm of her callused fingers. Even with all those extra eyes, it never looks back.

is a painter from Tierra del Fuego, educated in Paris, her supple fingers trying out tones instead of hues, her husband asleep on the veranda. She made her fortune in oysters and sheep, and her husband, who married for money, learned to stay for love. And for love of a sleeping man she abandons her grandmother's piano in the parlor for the ebony desktop that her grandfather shipped around the horn. The lump of potato that hunches in front of her fingers grew in the servants' garden out back. Lupita scrubbed it blind until the starchy white of its soul shone through. If the artist were playing at the real piano she would play Satie. Here, at the ebony desk, her fingers play the surf breaking in from Antarctica, the glitter of the Southern Cross, the huddle of shorn sheep against the leeward wall of a lambing shed. Her blue silk shift blows about her in the breeze, and the sibilant caress of her fingers on the desktop wakes something symphonic in the dreams of her husband. He sweeps the paper keyboard aside and lifts her shift and loves her there as he has not loved her in years, and she lets her faithful blind potato watch.

is not a woman yet but a village girl from Nebaj with black sapphire eyes, a muddied slat across her knees, two octaves marked out with stick-scratches and charcoal. She hums a scrap of tune to the *pitta-ta pitta-ta* tapping of fingertips on thin white pine. The small potato between her bare feet stands on end on the ground. More than half of its eyes watch the flicker of her fingers and the tight purse of her chapped lips. She frowns at the potato, and the potato trembles with the pulse of blood through her feet or with joy from the thrill of her playing. This girl heard piano for the first time on her uncle's radio that he bought at Chichi that time the army fought the army in the Church of God's Grandmother. Her uncle and the old witch-woman from La Libertad hid from the fighting behind a carving of God's Mother, and the *bruja* sold him that little radio while they waited for enough soldiers to be dead to stop shooting. The girl's wide, dark eyes focus on the music within, never see the desperate potato trying to applaud without hands.

loves a deaf man from Nanaimo, and doesn't need a piano. Some nights, when he is away driving truck, she wants him to call and sometimes he feels this and he does call. He speaks to the same silence whether she answers or not. But those other nights she waits up, tired but sleepless after waiting tables, and practices deaf piano for him in the kitchen, where she drew a keyboard on the yellow formica with a blue felt pen. Mu used to jump onto the table to bat at the flurry of her fingers, but he died Monday morning on the highway out back. Saturday night one unwashed Idaho spud rocks in a basket on the tabletop, oblivious to everything but those long, black fingers marking time until the woman's deaf man drives up at dawn for his sausage, his eggs over easy and his plate of fresh hash browns.

WALKING THE WHITMAN MISSION

Step east, into their shadows.
Stand with cottonwoods at your back
and hold your breath as they hold theirs.

Listen for screams stuttering
through the crumbling memories of stones.

Kneel here between ruts
push your hand deep into mud.
Your pulse echoes the westering throb
of wheels and oxen, axes.

Winds off the Blue Mountains
ripple ryegrass, your hair
a thin harvest of faces in a pond.

Turn your back to the sentry on the hill.
He strikes the air with feathers
and drums out the fever in his eyes.
Behind him, a clatter of dried bones
scatters like wings.

One magpie struts and pokes
at bright red splashes in the leaves.

The mud on your hand flakes off.
Those white feathers of your breath
twirl like hope in clean winter air.

WAR BABY

I was a three-day pass in San Francisco.
Her only time on a train, Mom rode
down, and she and I rode back. Hot
Quonset hut; drunk sailors and their brides
waited in line. Skinny little tipsy Mom
with Dad the Navy's middle-weight
champ, ship-sinker, screamer in the night.
He never expected me. After the war,

I was the accident he met at the door.
The battleship of our lives deployed into perpetual
winter. He'd expected to die, imagined my tiny
mother cashing his claim, regular grief her tribute, his
graveside memory honorable and enduring. Imagine
his surprise when he lived. Imagine his impossible
mission. Imagine paradise, that last three-day pass,
safe and drunk with a good woman in his home port.

SLUG

Old leopard-skin hermaphrodite
  hangs a dangle of slime
    from a slip of salal, and swings
      down the wind to those querying

        eyestalks of his glistening *her*.
    She's the *she* this time, so he
      lifts her off the trail, she clasps
        foot-to-foot, top-to-bottom, pas de
          deux slower now they're heavier
          in the wind and they begin that
          ancient wrap of skins, that slow,
        wet-skin writhe that births us all.

        Moonrise, finally, they stretch and
    slide back up the trail. Now, night and
      their silver alphabet, this living calligraphy,
      shimmers under our ivory moon.

MEETING DAD

Today we get our own place through the hedge and next to the store.

"You get to meet your daddy today," Grandpa says. "We saved one of your fish for his dinner tonight."

My daddy's coming home from the war. He's a sailor. Grandma says wars are very noisy. The sawmill where Grandpa works is very noisy. The men talk with their hands all the way across the mill because you can't hear. We take Grandpa his lunch every day when we hear the big saw shut down. I already know signs for "bread" and "roast beef" and "beer." Grandma won't let them talk with their hands at home. She tells them, "Go wash those dirty hands if you're sitting at my table," even if they just washed them.

Mom says my dad talks with his hands, too, but Grandma shakes a finger and says, "Not in front of the boy."

"You're quiet this morning," Grandpa says. "Are you worried about moving?"

I'm not worried. Mom looks at the paper and worries. She listens to the radio and worries and she worries when she gets mail. She worries when she doesn't get mail. Worry is sitting at the table crying. I'm not crying.

"Maybe you're worried about meeting your dad."

"I'm not worried," I say.

"Oh, so you *can* talk." He butters the hot toast and sits down to dip.

"People who kill in wars, can they kill anywhere?"

"No," he says, "just in the war, and the war's over." He takes a big bite of hot coffee and toast and breathes fast to cool it down. "You'll just be through the hedge there. We even made you a tunnel. Now eat."

After breakfast, we go see the tunnel through the hedge. I carry paintbrushes and tape in a bag for Grandpa. He skipped work today so somebody else has to start the saw. The train with people always rattles the house a little bit before the mill whistle blows. Grandpa starts the big saw after the train and just before the whistle. That big saw whines on down the street and Grandma says, "There he is. There's your Grandpa."

Sheep live in the lumber yard at the mill to keep the grass neat. The people train isn't here yet. He carries the cans of paint for our new walls.

"You can pull your wagon through here," Grandpa says.

I can almost stand up straight in the tunnel.

"We should've used your wagon to haul this paint."

My mother sings *Our room, our room* and dances us around our next-door home. My aunt and my cousin Philip have the same home across the wall. Creaky, creaky stripey floor we shine with our socks. Philip got too tired sliding with our socks. He got real blue and couldn't breathe very well, so he has to lie down for awhile.

We have a window we have an icebox we have ice. Wet stinging ice, icebox wet metal smell. Big handle *click click.*

Don't get in there stay out of there little boys hurt in there did you like the parade all the flowers? The nice girl gave you a flower?

This picture on top of the icebox is my dark dad in his white sailor suit, and another in his boxing trunks with his boxing gloves, and another in his dark sailor suit with my Mom all dressed up. The boxing glove picture has scary eyes.

Grandpa made me a chest out of lumber from the mill with two drawers. I get to put away my own clothes. The ones I'll wear to church Mom hangs up with hers in the ironing-board closet. Grandpa and Grandma set our bed against the wall and another little bed against the other wall by my two drawers. The aunts all of the women here with blankets our yellow curtains a table. The aunts nail up a clothesline and hang a green sheet between our bed and the little bed. Curtains and table and flower all yellow and green window open. Grandma stands me on the table, points out the windy window.

"Out there," she says, "train tracks and coalyard and trouble."

We get grain off the train tracks for Grandpa's chickens and pigeons. We get free coal off the train tracks for the heater.

Grandma calls the men on the train car *Trouble.*

Grandpa says if she wouldn't feed them, they wouldn't come to the door.

"They're every one of them somebody's boy," she says.

Grandpa pipe smoke smells and coffee, radio squeaks smells hot then "Four-Leaf Clover" music and the women dance. Grandpa bobs us on his knee: "Billy McGee of the horse marines he feeds his horse on pork and beans." Grandma fries baloney on the camp stove and the women and my soft mother dance.

I wake up on the little bed in the dark. Light under the door to the kitchen. My Mom laughs and ice tinkles a glass. One aunt says, "there's headlights! They're here!" Another aunt says, "Get the boy, his daddy's here!"

The light hurts my eyes, and Philip grabs my arm.

"C'mon, wake up! Our dads are here!"

Everybody's in our kitchen, yelling and patting backs and kissing. One man's face is bandaged, and one has dark black hair. My dad's the one with black hair. Philip's dad with the bandaged face tries to lift him, but can't.

"I'll be tossing you to the rafters in no time," he says, and kisses Philip's hair.

My black-haired dad is kissing my Mom so hard she can't breathe. She turns red, not blue like Philip. He bends her over backwards. She hits my dad's shoulder and he stops.

"Meet your son," she says.

He looks down, laughs.

"So, this is the boy," he says. He sticks his hand out, his big boxing hand. "Glad to meet you."

My Mom slaps his arm. "You're kidding! He's your *son*." She turns to me and motions me toward him. "Come here and give your father a kiss."

He's very big and has the whisky smell that Grandma hates. His hand on my chest. I stop. Then he reaches his boxing hand out again.

"Men don't kiss men," he says. "Men shake hands."

Mom says, "Oh, for Pete's sake!" And everyone gets quiet.

So I shake hands with my dad and Mom hands him and my uncle a drink. We get some cake. Then Grandpa and Grandma walk me through the hedge and let me camp on the couch with the radio. "Four Leaf Clover" comes on again and Grandpa's pipe smoke from the porch and Grandma crying.

"I hope she knows what she's getting into," Grandma says. "I hope she can handle it."

Grandpa says something quiet. Grandma stops crying, he knocks his pipe out on the step, and they *creak-creak* up the stairs to bed.

BUMBLEBEES

Billy! My little sister screams *Billy!* from the curb
her curly hair and her saggy diaper abuzz with bees.

I toss my listless grasshopper and scramble gravel
to the dry, dusty grasses across the road.

A sizzle of bumblebees streams from the ground
grabs us both with their stiff, stickery legs, and stings.

All around us their sweet, fresh dust of pollen
beats the summer air to a thick, yellow shimmer.

Scoop up sister, bumblebees and all, and *sting!* right
between the eyes. Face puffs tight, forehead nearly splits

births this pale mole. My shaving mirror adds twin silver hairs.
Her little fingers clutch my neck tight even now: *Billy!*

LEAVING DAD

We kids who ride the city bus walk to the bus stop past a man setting buckets of golf balls along a covered boardwalk inside a fenced field. Big fishnets ripple in the wind on top of the high board fence. Every afternoon on our way home we pass a line of men whacking golf balls into the nets. Markers on the grass tell them how far they hit. Some of the balls punch through the holes or pop over the nets. We like to cut them open to see who can unwind the whole rubber band without breaking it. Golf balls work pretty good in a slingshot, too, but I still prefer banana slugs. If we don't have anything better to do after school, we make fun of the golfers. We climb up on the ledge of the Nalley's Potato Chip sign, which puts us above the wood fence and behind the nets. Then we jump up and down and dare them to hit us. The owner likes this because all the men immediately start hitting balls like crazy. They lob quite a few over the nets, off the sign and into the lot below. So one day after school the owner stops me.

"Hey," he says, and motions me over. He's outside the fence with a bucket picking up the stray balls. "Are you that fighter's kid?"

At school that line always means somebody wants to fight *me*. Adults are mostly just curious.

"Yeah."

He sets the bucket of balls inside the gate beside several other full buckets.

"Does he golf?"

"I don't think so."

"What about his buddies?" he asks. "Any of those guys golf?"

"I don't think so."

He frowns, purses his lips and crosses his arms like somehow he's worried about that.

"You have some of the best athletes in town right back there in the projects, and nobody golfs." He shakes his head. "I don't get it."

I point to his *1 bucket of balls $1* sign and say, "We don't have a dollar."

"Hm," he says.

Some men inside the field holler for him to hurry it up with the balls. He frowns deeper and shakes his head again. Then he points his finger in the air like he's got a great idea, and he laughs. "Hey, kid, you want a job?" He reaches around the open gate and hands me four empty buckets. "Pick up the balls outside the fence, and I'll give you a quarter a bucket."

At least fifty buckets' worth of balls are scattered under the Nalley's Potato Chip sign, and these four buckets make a dollar right here right now. Dad made $25 fighting at the armory last week. I can make that much picking up golf balls. The golf guy is gone already delivering his buckets, so I get busy. I fill the four buckets really fast and get a quarter each time I bring one in. I hurry home so Mom doesn't worry. Grandma gave me a pig bank with a plug in its belly so I don't have to break it to get my money out. I have $7.10 from saving my milk money and helping Grandpa stack firewood. My quarters *clinkle clinkle clinkle clinkle* into my pig and make $8.10.

"Mom! Mom! I have a job and I already made a dollar!"

"A job?" She laughs. "What kind of job?"

I tell her about the fifty buckets of balls waiting to be picked up.

"How come Dad and the other guys don't golf? The golf guy says they're the best athletes and they don't golf."

Mom sits at the table with me and frowns at her coffee.

I tell her, "I told him we didn't have a dollar for a bucket of balls."

She raises her eyebrows. "That's God's own truth," she says. "But you know that most of the fighters here are Negroes. Ever see a Negro man golf there?"

I haven't.

"Ever see a woman of any kind golf there?"

"No."

"He doesn't like some people even if they have a dollar." She lights a cigarette and lets me blow out the match. "But you pick up your fifty buckets and get your quarters. How much will you get for fifty buckets?"

She likes me to do math problems with money. Four buckets makes one dollar, so forty makes ten dollars. Ten more buckets is two dollars and a half, so:

"Twelve dollars and fifty cents."

"That's big money," she says, and sips her coffee. "I want you to stay outside the fence, okay? I don't want you going in there with those men. He just wants you to work outside, anyway, right?"

"Yes. He just wants the ones that go outside the fence."

Right away after school Garn invites me in to hit a bucket of balls.

"On the house," Garn says. "Let's see your swing."

"I can't."

"You got an appointment? Of course you can."

He holds the side gate open for me. Two guys are hitting balls. They're on each end of a long stage that has twelve places to hit balls. The closest guy pours a bucket of balls into a chute, and they pop up in front of him one by one as he whacks them into the downfield net.

"I'm not making any money today anyway, so what the hell? C'mon, hit a bucket on me."

I can't tell him that my mother told me to stay outside the fence. That's sissy stuff. And lying's a sin.

"Okay," I say, "but I have to get home and watch my sister."

"Hey, I'm not keeping you. I just thought you'd like to try it after watching these guys every day. C'mere, let's find you something to swat with."

I follow him through the gate and up the steps behind the front counter. The back room is packed with boxes of candy bars, pop, cigarettes and golf balls. Golf clubs line the walls behind the counter like we did for our school picture—short ones in front and big ones in the back. He picks out three of the short clubs, lights a cigarette and squints at a bucket of balls.

"Grab that," he says, and coughs. "I think we're set."

We wait for the first guy to finish his swing before we walk behind him to the second spot.

"Garn," the guy says, "I'll need another bucket here."

"Me, too," the other guy says. "I'm out down here."

Garn pours my balls into the chute and one pops up on a little stand in front of me.

"Hold on, hold on," he says. "I'm setting up the boy here."

He hands me a club with a big head and shows me how to hold it.

"Now whack a few while I get these men set up. I'll be right back."

My first swing hits the floor first and just bounces the ball off the edge of the stage. I look out at the numbers on the signs across the stretch of green—100, 200, 300, 400. The 400 is painted on the tall back fence. I went about 4.

"Here, kid," the guy next to me says, "hold it like this." He moves my hands down the club a little bit. "Now stand beside the ball and take a couple of practice swings before you go for the ball. Like this."

He shows me on his last ball and has to wait for more. I hit the next few balls pretty good. Garn sells each of the guys two more buckets, then four more guys come in and he gets busy. By the time I finish my bucket of balls I'm not hitting as hard but I'm hitting straighter, which the guy next to me says is most important.

"Hey, kid," he says, "fetch me a bucket and I'll give you a quarter." He hands me a dollar bill and a quarter.

Garn's real busy, so by the time I get back two more guys want me to run to the counter for them. I don't have to pick up all the balls to earn a quarter a bucket. I just have to run to the counter with the money and hurry full buckets back to the golfers. I make five dollars before it starts getting dark and I have to get home. Garn says this might work out regular for me if I can find somebody to pick up the balls outside the fence. Inside the fence he drives a thing like a huge vacuum cleaner that sucks up the balls into big canvas bags that fill up most of his back room. I can't find anyone in our neighborhood whose Mom would let him pick up balls at the driving range, so I have to keep doing that. After I'm done with that, then I can run buckets for the guys. It's not so bad, but I get home late and my Mom doesn't like it.

"I want you home earlier," she says. "You're too tired doing your homework."

My pig bank's already overfull. Besides running for buckets of balls, I run for cigarettes, Cokes, candy bars. Sometimes they give me a candy bar instead of money. I put the candy bar back in the case and take out fifteen cents on my way home. The candy in that case is so old that I think I've traded in the same candy bar every time. I could keep them for Maude, but I'd rather have the money. I have enough now for a bike for me and a trike for her. I trade in my quarters for paper dollars, and when I run buckets I never get less than a five-dollar bill, so I have almost two hundred dollars. In fact, I only need three dollars and a quarter to make that two hundred. I'm just running up to the counter to get two buckets and a pack of Lucky Strikes for Mr. Gallagher when dad walks in. I'm filling Mr. Gallagher's buckets from a barrel in the back behind the counter, so I duck behind the barrel. Dad's wearing his sunglasses in the rain again, which means he has a fresh black eye.

"Hello, Bill," Garn says. "You got something for me?"

My dad slaps an envelope on the counter. Garn opens it, and I see a lot of money crammed inside. Garn counts it while Dad lights one of Garn's smokes. He looks around, and those sunglasses hide his eyes.

"It's not all here."

"He gave me what he had, and I took the rest out on his face."

"Looks like you paid a little interest yourself," Garn says.

He laughs, Dad doesn't. Garn pulls a bill out of the envelope and sets it on the counter.

"Wasn't hardly worth the bus ride," Dad says.

"I'll have something for you Friday night after the races," Garn says.

"I'm fighting at the Armory Friday night, a ten-round feature."

"It'll keep until Saturday, I'm sure."

"Saturday I'm bouncer at the Willows."

"So collect in the afternoon, bounce at night."

I've seen my dad fight, but I guess I've never seen him bounce. He always walks really smooth, like a leopard.

"Hey, if your boy on Saturday gets rough like this one did, then I'll lose the bouncer job. Can't have a guy all beat up at the door, bad for business. I'll do it Sunday. I'll do it while the wife and kids are at church."

"That adds two days' interest," Garn says. "We both make a little more for our trouble—" Mr. Gallagher bumps my dad aside at the counter.

"Hey, Garn! Where's that kid with my balls and my smokes? I gotta get back to—hey, there he is."

Everything stands still. I let out the breath I'm holding, pick up the two full buckets and set them beside Mr. Gallagher. I reach behind the counter for his Luckies and hand him back his money. Nobody says anything, and nobody moves. I walk straight out the side gate and straight home. Mom's at work, and Nurse Rusty, the red-haired county health nurse, watches Maude who has whooping cough. She has her blanket and her toys and doesn't move at all. I got scared when I had it and couldn't breathe, but I get more scared when Maude can't breathe. She passes out and gets blue. She's not blue now, but she sure looks tired.

"Where's your dad?" Nurse rusty asks. "I can't hang around here all day."

"Right here," he says. He's huffing a little from running home. *"You!"* he says, pointing at me. "Take your sister and your butt into the back room and stay there."

"Don't be so rough on the boy," Nurse Rusty says.

"Keep out of this," my dad snaps.

I get Maude, her blanket and her toys into our bed in the back room. Sometimes she wets the bed, and she rolls over on my side to do it. Mom got her a plastic pad that I put under her, but it doesn't do much good when she rolls off it. I think, *if she can roll over to pee, she can get up to do it.* She's lucky, we had an outhouse when I was her age. Dad's still talking to Nurse Rusty in the living room. I get Maude and her things onto her pad and tucked in. I tuck extra tight on my side because she wets the bed more when she's sick. She starts coughing again, and then the whooping. I'm wanting Dad or Rusty to come check on her, but nobody's coming and she's whooping herself blue, now. Now she's not breathing. I run into the living room and yell, "Dad! Dad!" and Nurse Rusty jumps off my dad who jumps off the couch. They're both buck naked except for their socks. They both have white socks. Nurse Rusty has bright red hair between her legs that she grabs with one hand while she snatches up her uniform with the other.

"Get your ass in the back room *now!*" Dad yells.

I run to the back room and feel like I have to pee. My sister's breathing again, and she's not blue anymore. She's sweating and crying, with goo in her eyes. Dad busts in behind me, just wearing his shorts. He grabs me by the arm and shakes a finger in my face.

"Don't you say anything about this to anybody, you get me?"

"Yes."

He picks me up by the arm and shakes me against he wall.

"And you're not going back to that driving range, you get that, too?"

I can hardly breathe.

"Yes."

I'm starting to cry, and that will make things worse, but Nurse Rusty's in the doorway and she says, "Bill, put the kid down. You're scaring him to death. If you hurt him, I'll tell your wife myself. Walk me out."

That look from my dad, I know I'm dead. I saw it that time he beat that guy on the bus, and that night we came to pick him up at the Willows and the headlights caught my uncle holding a guy from behind while my dad beat him.

"Bill!"

He lets go my arm and I run to the bathroom and lock the door. He's yelling at Maude now to shut the fuck up. He's going to kill me, and I can't stay in the bathroom forever.

I wake up in the dark in the neighbor's car. Mom's driving. The engine's going really fast and we're going really slow. I've never seen Mom drive. She's crying, and she cries harder when people honk at her. My sister's asleep in the back seat, breathing really hard.

"Oh, thank God you're awake!"

Mom reaches over to touch me but I hurt all over and I don't want anybody to touch me.

"We're going back to Grandma and Grandpa's in the valley," she says. "I talked with Father O'Brien and they're opening the new school there. Some of the nuns from Visitation will be there, so you won't be a stranger."

She's not crying now, but her eyes are nearly swelled shut and her glasses are all messy. My sister coughs herself awake.

"And I've been waiting for the right time to tell you two, but this'll have to do," she says. "We're going to have a baby. You're going to have another little brother or sister."

"Sister," Maude says. "I already have a brother."

That's the most she's said in nearly a week.

"What about Dad?"

We're turning across the tracks now, down into my Grandparents' driveway. All the lights are on, and Grandpa stands on the porch, smoking his pipe, hands tucked under his suspenders.

"I hit him with the iron," she says. "That ought to hold him awhile."

My pig bank made it with me, but it's empty.

CATECHISM

The old nun hovers hooded, blue-eyed:
"What happens to those souls who take their own lives?"
Your gaze inspects your desktop.
"Stand when called upon!"
Your so-white hands shake like ginkgo leaves
breathless tears move you slowly to the door.

I sit, quiet as packed dirt.

"If you leave this room, keep on going."
Years behind those flooded eyes your father dangles
like a burnt moth from a noose in our old tree house.
Both of us keep on going.

TRILLIUM

Saturday morning my cousin Philip and I hunt trilliums for our Moms in the woods behind their house. We bring home a whole lunchbox full.

"Now they won't bloom again," Mom says. "Leave them be. We'll put these in water; they'll be fine for today. Now go back outside and play. Remember, no running with Philip."

We take our bows outside to shoot at the target my uncle set up on some hay bales. We can at least hit the bales every time. We get bored and Philip has the idea to put the target on the ground.

"This is like artillery," he says. "You shoot as straight up as you can and see how close you can drop onto the target."

I look at the target at our feet, at the sky, then at the house, barn, horses all in easy range.

"If we shoot straight up," I say, "maybe it'll come straight down and hit *us*."

"It's only one arrow," he says. "It can't hit both of us."

I put the target at the bottom of the hill, just to be sure, and we stand on top to get more height. We both shoot a few arrows, arcing closer to the target each time. This way the wild shots stick straight up out of the ground, a lot easier to find than our usual, buried under the brush. After my turn, I'm pulling my last arrow when Philip yells, "Look out! Look out!"

I jump up, and his arrow punches down into the bone of my left shoulder. The arrow sticks straight down, the shaft flicking my ear, and I drop to my knees in the dirt. The arrow rings when it hits bone, and that tone runs right up my collarbone and into my skull. My stomach's turning over. I try to get up, but the arrow weighs me down. Philip appears like magic, gasping.

"I'm sorry, I'm sorry," he says. "I just…wanted to get close enough…to scare you."

I feel funny, like nothing's connected, and can't talk.

"You're bleeding," he says. He tries pulling the arrow, but it doesn't come out. My shoulder itches really bad when he wiggles the arrow.

Philip skins off his t-shirt and holds it where the arrow goes in. That stops the bleeding while he catches his breath. His skinny chest and belly blotch blue and white as he struggles to breathe. A thick, blue scar down the middle marks where they saved him when he was born. He still has a hole in his heart that makes him blue, so he isn't supposed to run with us. His blue lips say something I can't hear. My hands feel tingly, and black spots swarm over everything.

Philip yanks hard this time. The arrow sucks out, and my breath comes back with a snort. Blood wells down my shirt every time my heart pounds. He wads his shirt up under my shirt to stop it. My blood smears his hands and chest.

"We're going to get in trouble," I say.

He grunts something and helps me up. My legs won't work right.

"We'll just go straight to my bedroom," he says. "We can clean up there."

This is my Mom's first visit to my dad's family since we left. My dad isn't here. Mom, my aunt and my uncle are playing Hearts in the kitchen with the radio blasting, so we sneak through there really fast to get to Philip's bedroom. Everything goes silent. Then the door bangs open, and the room fills with adults and shouting, and then I wake up at home on Sunday afternoon with a perfectly round hole where my collarbone meets my shoulder bone. Now it throbs, and when Mom changes the bandage I see the crusty yellow powder the doctor stuffed inside.

"It has to heal from the inside out," Mom says. "That powder keeps it from closing up too soon and getting infected."

"What did the Indians use?"

"They had their own powders." She puts on a fresh pile of gauze pads and tapes it into place. "Medicine men and women knew the right plants and how to use them. People here used Devil's Club root for diabetes. Grandma takes shots."

"They're both prickly."

My shoulder won't let my arm work right to get into a new t-shirt.

"Here," Mom says, "use this old shirt in case the bandage leaks."

My cousin's hand-me-down shirt from last year presses the bandage tight, and the sleeves come nowhere near my wrists. He's a year older, but a lot smaller.

"I can cut those off for you if you want," she says.

"I'll just roll them up."

Five hard knocks at the door.

Dad!

Mom sighs and makes a face.

"Don't worry," she says. "It wasn't your fault. I'll take care of it."

Dad looks different than I've ever seen him. He's *scared*.

"Philip's in the hospital," he says. "His heart gave out after everybody left. He wants to see the boy. I borrowed a car."

I haven't been alone with my dad since the divorce, and I really don't want to be alone with him.

"He didn't have to run," I say. "It didn't really bleed until later."

"Nobody's blaming you!" he snaps. He clears his throat. "Philip might not make it this time, and he wants to see you. Do you want to go?"

Might not make it! My legs and stomach feel like when the arrow hit.

"He can barely walk," Mom says. "I don't think he should go."

"I think he should. And I think we should get going *now*."

"That serious?"

"Yes."

I get my breath back.

"I want to see him," I say. "I have to show him my shoulder."

Dad and I practice not looking at each other while Mom helps me into my coat.

"I'll get him back tonight," he says. "It might be late. Philip's in Seattle."

Seattle is a long drive and Grandpa's car barely makes it up the hills, and the hospital is part of a school that's bigger than our town. My dad never says a word until we get to the hospital, and neither do I. We pass a room with kids in iron lungs. Last year we got shots so it wouldn't happen to us. We all know kids who left school with polio, and we heard about iron lungs that help them breathe, but I didn't imagine those coffins. The kids have mirrors tilted up in front of them so they can see who they're talking to on the out breath. Kids in braces and on crutches practice walking in the halls. Philip's room is on the top floor. The hallway sounds pump and beep, the *squeak-squeak* of nurses' shoes, the *thucka-thucka-thucka* of wheels on carts. Otherwise, everything's quiet.

"Your aunt and uncle went for a bite to eat," the nurse says. "Your cousin wanted to see you alone, is that okay?"

She asks me, but she looks at my dad.

We both say yes.

She squats down to my level.

"Your cousin's very, very sick," she says. "Because of that, and because of some medicines we've been giving him, he might not look the same, but it's him. Will you be okay?"

"What does he look like?"

"Well, basically he's just swelled up, kind of puffy."

"Oh."

"And he has a lot of trouble breathing. That's what the tube going to his nose is for, to give him oxygen. So if you ask him a question, you'll have to give him time to answer."

"Okay." I have no idea what I might ask him.

She pulls a curtain aside and says, "Philip, your cousin's here to see you." And she leaves.

He's very puffed up. I wouldn't recognize him except he laughs and wheezes, "Cochise."

"Geronimo," I say. "What's the plan?"

"Save yourself," he says. "I'm only...going out...feet first."

"Not funny."

"True."

He catches his breath for a second, and I take the chair beside his bed. A pitcher of water and a glass with a straw sit on the bedside stand.

"Want some water?" I ask.

He wheezes another laugh and puts a weak hand to his puffy face.

"This is...all water. Hey. That's...my shirt."

"Looks a lot better on me."

"Makes you...look better...you mean."

He closes his eyes for a moment and concentrates on breathing.

"Shoulder?"

"Just a little hole with some powder in it. Want to see?"

"Yeah."

I unbutton the shirt and peel back the bandage. He can barely turn his head, so I have to lean real close. His breathing gurgles and pops against my neck.

"Cool...sorry."

He closes his eyes and sinks back into his pillow.

"It's okay," I say. "I'm the only kid in town who's been shot with a real arrow."

Philip tilts his head back to breathe easier.

"I scared…a nurse."

"How'd you do that?"

"Student…nurse," he says. "I quit…breathing…stared straight."

"What'd she do?"

He wheezes another laugh. "Ran…yelled, 'Code Blue!'"

"But you're always blue."

"Yeah. Perfect…huh?"

He laughs, then seems to sleep for a few seconds, snoring in quick breaths. His eyes are closed and I'm ready to call the nurse when he speaks.

"Your school?" he asks. "They teach you…about God?"

I feel a chill take my spine. I know then for sure that Philip is going to die. My dad's family doesn't go to church. We never talk to them about being Catholics, and we never talk about God. And his tone of voice is dead serious.

"They teach us that different people have different ideas of God, but that they're all trying to get at the same thing."

He doesn't say anything. I listen to his breathing for awhile, then the snoring sound comes back, then he says, "You…know me. Will I… go…to Hell?"

I know what the Church would say, that he has to be baptized to go to Heaven. But I can't imagine God turning Philip away.

"Be straight…Cochise."

"The Church says we're the image and likeness of God," I say. "That means he's got a sense of humor. I'd say you're in."

His eyes open as best they can through those puffy lids.

"I stole…pop. I lied…I swore…I looked…at Tim's…dirty pictures."

This time he keeps his gaze on me while he catches his breath.

"God wouldn't care about that stuff," I say. "You didn't kill anybody, did you?"

I'm stalling, stalling for something right to say.

"Didn't…have time."

Then I think of something Father O'Brien said: *Anyone can baptize anyone else in an emergency.*

"This is an emergency," I whisper.

"No shit…Sherlock," Philip whispers back.

I try to think of what Father O'Brien would say. I go to confession to him because he's fast and doesn't lecture.

"Are you sorry for the things you did that you think were wrong?" I ask.

The answer is "Yes" in a long heavy sigh.

I take the glass of water and trickle it over his head.

"I baptize you in the name of the Father and of the Son and of the Holy Ghost, amen."

"That's…better," he says. He still looks me in the eye, but now his breath comes in huge sighs. Then, "You," he laughs, "a…priest."

Then, he simply never takes a breath in. I wait, put the water glass back, wait some more because he pulled this one already on the nurse. But then I can see he isn't in there. I can't touch him. All I can think to say is, "I won't forget you."

Something must've gone off somewhere because a lot of nurses come running in and one pushes me out into the hall with Dad.

"You all right?" he asks.

"Yes."

"What did he say?"

"He wanted to know about God."

"And I suppose you told him all about it."

That's his picking a fight voice that he gets when we talk about God.

"Yes."

He's about to say something when one of the nurses comes out and shakes her head. Dad sighs.

"What did he say," he asks, "when you told him?"

I don't want to say anything about baptizing anybody.

"He said, 'That's better,'" I say, "then he laughed."

"He *laughed*?"

Dad squints at me and shakes his head. "Well I'll be go-to-hell."

He pats me twice on the back, the first time he's touched me since the split, and we head to the cafeteria to break the news to my aunt and uncle.

SHOOTING THE THIEF

Fifteen, I stumble home after midnight from the cannery,
too double-shifted to smell the sweet-grass at the river
or the bread rising in my aunt's bakery next door.

I don't need light to find my bed on the back porch,
I need out of these berry-soaked clothes and into bed.
My pants hit the floor. I hear a ratchet *zip zip zip*.

I peel curtains aside like a bandage. A shadow of a thief
hunches over my mother's tires, her battery and generator
that she bought with her sweat and cracked, bleeding hands.

I load the old single-shot 12-gauge and snick shut the breech,
hold my breath and ease open our thin back door. He's smaller
than his shadow. I tap him on the shoulder with the muzzle.

"Hey, fucker," I say, and he runs. Without a grunt or a look,
he jumps up and runs. This isn't the way of things in the movies.
He's supposed to put up his hands, say he's sorry, wait for the police.

The dark blob of him nearly makes the tracks when I split the night with fire
that brings Mom, my sisters, the neighbors, the cops. My thief shows up
at the hospital to get the lead out, winds up doing seven years.

The cop, my ex-dad's ex-partner, says I have to go downtown.
"Stripping cars ain't a capital offense," he says. "Here's the rule:
If we can't hang'em, you can't shoot'em." He lets me go at dawn.

PUYALLUP RIVER

In Memoriam: Annie Marcoe

Clumsy dog snorts in the fog, out of focus where the willow
stand many years shorter; somewhere a muddy sack
swells with traps, scarred salmon and muskrat hides.

I watch myself in the fog—dull, nearsighted trudge—
shoulder the sack up there by the bend, wipe my nose
on my crusty sleeve, slip into the dark past the droopy trees.

The dog licks my hand and the river runs older. Tears
are stones in this singing water, and a strange swamp-thickness
glows through that soft old river in my bones.

SACRIFICE

Too long a sacrifice can make a stone of the heart. –W.B. Yeats

We stare into the same wilderness, into the shards
that were our smiles, our touch, our precious memory.

Divine symmetry uncoils, unbends its vortices and roots,
scribes an arc across the night with you, sleeping, there,
and me, not quite lost (okay, lost) over here.

At dawn, make promises to dirt. Remember what holds you up
and what even the most pragmatic bones become.

THE CENTER

What is truth? –Pontius Pilate

A talking skull on the tip of a spear
faces West, shrieks with the night wind:

*If they do these things in a green tree
what shall they do in a dry?*

A one-eyed dog whines below,
licks the sores of any beggar.
These two, and a cracked lamp
keep watch in the square.

Shadows in our own homes,
we flicker like black tongues
behind our curtains and flimsy plank doors.

*If they do these things in a green tree
what shall they do in a dry?*

There are no children here.
The smooth path around the skull
wears deeper every year,
the sand in the center grows darker.

We would leave
but there are so few of us
and the distance from the center is so great.

MOTHER

screams in my dream and snaps me into our darkest hour.
Phone at dawn, long drive through forest and fog,
this bitter bite of antiseptic on the air answer everything
the blind receptionist doesn't ask. I read tests to her
in high school. She knows my voice, points the way.

doesn't hurt now, wants me beside her when the doctor comes.
He comes early, swiping at tears, his voice tight as a teenager's.
"In your liver," he says. "A month…outside…."
One measly measure of moon, a whittling away of light, then night.
"Get me some cigarettes," she whispers. "They won't kill me now."

rides home in the ambulance we stole to steal her with, laughing,
picks out her coffin from a catalogue and the pillow from samples.
"Next best thing to a doctor in the family," she tells her son-in-law,
the mortician. "Just do me two favors: don't take out my teeth,
and don't play with my teats."

can't get to the bathroom, so I carry those tiny bones wrapped
in thin, bruised skin. Her husband drinks and gripes. She confesses
she hates him. Asks for Dad alone, who leaves crying. Asks for a priest.
She laughs at the two new calves frisking the neighbor's pasture.
Then this thing she refuses to name takes her past knowing whether
that splinter of morning moon will rise and fill for anyone ever again.

Orientation 2.

A leg by itself is heavier than you'd think.

BUILDING

Pull that old crosscut down
set the mangled teeth and file them true.

Grow in tree-time. Simple as wood
as the bucking of wood, grow.

Too big finally for the sink, the crinkling
gray washtub, the house: split wood
and stack it. Morning blood crackles
crisp as the fresh white heart of alder.

One more stick in the stove and
coffee throats its low groan. Bed
in the corner moans, Table and Chair
sway and rustle like moss in the dark.
This pencil leans for water.

A GIFT POEM

McKenna Creek creeps west, shallow and slow as swamp.
Mist rises early, like Bigfoot, and loafs the day in secret
somewhere near the coast. Fishline *thlips* the water.

This land feels our footsteps.
Two dried snail shells rattle

my creel, barter for my daughter.
Signal when you're moving on.
I'll reel in a series of record dreams, and follow.

LEDA

The air between us thickens and dries.
     Give me a sign.
The hot of your breath is a feather.
Your words are feathers. The trill of your father:
a great gray quill nesting in the down of your first song.
     That will not do. A sign.
Here. Your hand. The pulse of sky itself.
Camellia blossoms whistle in the South Wind.
Use your wings.
     What is this smoothness between my legs?
The egg. Oh, sister, use your wings.
It is the egg.

LAKE KAPOWSIN

Morning fog conjures the lake a woman,
fleshes her pale foot beneath my door.

Step in, step in. I stretch awake.
Turn your back, dry your eyes.

I pull on armor, shrink from the chill. She faces
the window. Outside, one blue heron honks.

Flying blind? Want some breakfast?
This woman of fog won't speak.

Perfect nails comb out tangles of mist. She dissolves
with a word like love starting to her lips.

Call her love, luck, spirit or fog: she's gone.
Except for this nightly cold that noses my neck

while I sit to lamplight in my gray custom,
giving away my life here one sheet at a time.

FROM THE PORCH AT KAPOWSIN

Two shots punctuate a new flight of teal
and wind makes a river of the lake.

This rising moon is a last fistful of sun
jammed in the face of that hard night sky.

FISHING THE YELLOWJACKET

A fresh damp snakeskin uncurls,
one last slither wheezes out.

The Cascades creak open,
their rumpled backs bank this low fire.

Two gray salamanders scrape and skitter,
playing tag. Or loving. Or hunting.

Even before the first crisp light
stone flies dapple the water.

We shuck our thick night skins and glide
prehensile, across that long blue dawn.

WATERFRONT CAFÉ

A cedar wind off the islands curls through this fog
like a handful of hill. Sand fleas rustle under
long whips of kelp and waves lick cracked planks like arrows.

The woman who spills my coffee clunks through her morning
an unfendered boat at moorage. She slips off her glasses.
The tide pulls her through the window.

Fog sweeps her across the islands, pushes a listing gill-netter
desperately to sea. She turns, sighs, dusts her driftwood,
folds and stacks her unmatched napkins.

A loose log rolls in the surf outside.
Waiting, like we are waiting.

WORKING

The Lord deal kindly with you, as ye have dealt with the dead.
—Naomi

Nothing is harder than the work of the dead. Not
the finest African stone, not time, not
even the hot hot core of an imploding star.

> *Uh, us? Well, we're on relief.*

Scratch at walls in the ears
of the memories of the dead.

> *Somebody's got to shave 'em. Beard grows*
> *after you're gone, you know. Good money in it.*

The dead. We die with them.

> *Every time you pull somebody over*
> *you know they can blow you away*
> *soon's you step up to the car.*

Step up to the word, and the word
blows over you like the last leaf.

> *Gospel preachin's come and go,*
> *come and go. Been some time since*
> *anybody left grain on purpose for the gleaners.*

I plow the wind.

QUILCENE CAFÉ

On the porch, the candy-vendor holds his
breath like fog deep between his crumpled ribs.

Quick eyes crackle dry and brown, his good
shoulder bunches high against his chair.

Our waitress tucks his blankets close,
tugs and smoothes his rumpled coat.

She rustles like a deer through her pantry,
shuffles to our table like a bear.

His white breath, an uncoded message
bursting like dogwood in the shattering air.

CHIMACUM CAFÉ

Y'know how history repeats itself? –fellow customer

Talk of surgeries and recoveries drones like idling diesels.
Kidney displays and hog feed rub shoulders at the counter.
A network of scars grins from names that everybody knows but me:

Whadda you do, buddy?
He smirks at shadows of calluses shrinking behind my palms.

"Fisherman."
Hah! Whadda ya fish for? Compliments?

Gotta laugh. "Yep."
Well, boy, y'got damn nice handwriting.

His soft laugh rings with the doorbell:
silver spin of a quarter on his clean white plate.

PASTIME CAFÉ

Eyes in this place droop
thick puckers under the eyes
folds under necks droop
jowls and the plants in the windows
droop plants in the pictures on the walls
droop cigars in racks, bowling trophies
unmatched silver droops, this table
and its cracked vinyl chairs droop
warm salads, year-old crackers droop
my tired hands droop, Eddy Arnold
droops from the jukebox,
I wake up away from you again
and my whole body droops.

COFFEE AT LOW TIDE

Behind the café, sand fleas flick in the glare
and a dead gull's bones click together in the wind.

Mother moon's secret fingers peel the tide back and
the eye of noon parches the succulence out of things.

My chapped ears barely justify the ticklings
of their own stiff hairs.

Hairs bristle the frayed ends of kelp, curl around
their thin selves and quaver together in the spume.

The sea leaves corpses at my door:
bones and kelp and dead flies zizzing in a rusty can.

This dirge I toss back over coffee
as the tide in my dry eyes turns.

SOL DUC IN JULY

Down at the lake they're delicate as gnat-wings,
pudgy as polliwogs, gangly as herons or cranes.

The women wading discover hot mud.

Its sweet gush between toes
squinches their ecstatic eyes shut.

WINTER KILL

Across the fence, one winter rose yellows
the moon's bare garden at midnight.
The acid whiff of opened-up game shadows my back.

One of these days I'll drop out here, limp
as the neck of a dead goose,
asprawl my dreams and a half-black moon.

Yes, better to die snarled in beauty,
dizzy with incense and a full belly.
Better to live.

MARKING BOUNDARIES

They stare at you, would run from me.
Great brown ears fan, noses bob lightly at the wind.

You step in a slow dance, they step in a slow dance.
All of you balance in this ballet of bones and hoof
and shuffle of heavy clothes falling:

One whitetail flicker and your tentative wave
from past the crest of the first hill.

I turn back to dig an outhouse hole,
lay proper claim to the land.

Somewhere on the lee side of the last hill
an older claim lies steaming in the grass.

BURYING THE DOG
–for Bob and Hank

We sit the grave's damp rim and
skitter gravel down the slumping sides.
A light westerly nudges rain and evening
back against the trees. The bottle
passes around, around again.

Those younger dogs thrash shadows
out of the blackberry meadow. Wild rose
and the promise of that last stiff stink
hover close. Filling a grave
takes less breath than digging one.

STATE OF THE UNION

The heart of our beast, thicker
than a banker's waist, dark as treason—
what we bred with gold and fear.

That bloody crumple of lives in the news,
the heady whiff of our great beast's table
promise blood and a whiff of hot meat.

We huddle over grates in the street
empty wrappers of our days skitter past.

What holds us here sweeps us up,
stale scraps from some great feast.

HUNGER

The last curse of a shot dog
all snarl, gray lips and blood.

One arrowhead washes itself
at the well-side of coals

and red coals well in those yellow eyes
yonder, brimming the night's dark cup.

Orientation 3.

Dead babies, no matter what killed them,
wake you for the rest of your nights.

THE DARK

My bed sighs. In the morning I'll quit this
waving arms at the blind.

I need to be a wrecker driver
get out of construction for a season.

Try on new wives, new children,
union meetings once a month, beer and pizza
negotiations, sick leave, vacation.

Something doesn't suit me the way
dawn muscles in on my self-pity.

THE POSSESSED

The quiet mouth of our darkness opens like a stolen egg.
All the singing of the night unfolds inside.

Morning is a thin gnaw of silence, stumbling hungry through the trees.
A close brush of leaves prickles the quiet in an old crow's eye.

The swell of this day glows under a warm red cavity of sky,
a babble of small tongues grows, and casts us spinning to our trances.

INFESTED

Those angels on my toilet are getting me down.
Who can count how many preen and primp at my mirror?
They're like feathered wheels with an infinity of eyes.
The mirror only makes it worse.

They flush and flush all night, never shut off the shower
and steam themselves into a fluff over the sink. I think
it's the water. No plumbing in the seventh heaven,
and I know how that can be.

I'm not unzipping in front of cherubs, that's a fact,
and the water bill's atrocious. I buy privacy for a quarter
at the state park, but those seraphim keep crowding in.
Shit, here comes the landlady, and now they decide to sing.

DREAMING US LOST IN THE MOUNTAINS

High air whistles its thin bones between rocks
and bends the one bunch of grasses down.

A pair of nighthawks strains at their wings
outfluttering the few fat moths.

We bed down here in this gully, hum lullabies
and finger the stops in the flute of our night.

LETTER FROM THE ROAD

After winding through the Wasatch range
pull up at Bear River for a breather.
Late fall, and the Utah sun still fingers
one old brown hunkered deep in a deep pool.

Compare that trout to Life, to God,
to Love. *That's* poetry.

Lie. God manages well, and love, wily,
strong and sleek as a dream, is no fish.

Disappear, leave behind that one change of clothes,
maps, car. Slip into hills where rock meets rock
and death means one more sigh inside the wind.

Bend to drink: these pines whisper *No, no, not yet*
and everything nearby lies still. Sunset reddens a Kennecott sky
and the brown nuzzles nymphs from the bottom.
Look upstream; the future.

Think about the turns that love will take and
that long drive unravelling the highway home.

KOLOB CANYON

Something like wind rasps this gulch between us,
carves our red faces raw, lifts these wretched feathers of talk away.

It...*listen*:

Whips the blackest words of our lives across the sage
and prickly pear, and gone. Tonight, even where you sleep

old white-eye moon wanes.

NOTE TO A DISTANT WOMAN

Dawn, and an easy sweep of song and broom dances me around
and around the house. One shuddering sneeze blasts an ecstasy
of dust motes and droplets sifting breathless and still on the philodendron.

Later, the *hump* and *hunk* that spirit the ax center the woodcutting
and the wood. The sweet heart of cedar scents my hands, the air
and a few wild dreams of love that linger at the edges of things.

Tonight, all these old notebooks brim with the light of you
unblind the moth in me, turning pages, turning, turning to sleep.

MAPPING THE INTERIOR

...bearing with him the beast's face and the dream. –Loren Eiseley

You winter behind my brittle touch
and I learn to believe you real as stone.

This time of year the ice thins and clears.
These bones that whiten under my hide

turn to you nightly like needles in some
distant compass tight in the hand of the dead.

CONVERSATION

Owls in these hills own the words.
Trees up and down the gulch,
thistles, iris and wild rose wait out the centuries
with baskets of words under their petals and leaves.

They pray for the miracle of lips and mouths and tongues.

Distance glistens from the corners of your eyes
and all those words I've studied so well
steal from me and hide far and wide in the night.

Now, with all the ages of darkness shouting between us
even the oldest star is not telling anything it knows.

SEMAPHORE

I stepped carefully over her shadow as I walked away. –Loren Eiseley

The articulate light of our bones
pulses in the night like old scars.

A breathless sky bends down in silence
in a thin curve of quiet

and bridges the edges of our lives
mute and homely in their shivering skins.

INTERLUDE AT THE ACE OF CUPS
in A minor

Music from the coffeehouse waves sunset back
into the blue-black eyebrows of the hills.
A carver in the corner chips out lovers.
The customer beside her stirs his chocolate
and a soft bloom of hot milk lulls
his eyelids down, and he nods.

The one sunny day before solstice, and now
as evening clears, Gemini sends a stream
of meteors down the broadening night.
The customer wakes and wonders at his hands,
those wiry women who finish off his arms.
A last quiver of guitar hides itself in the dark.

The carver huddles tight to her work
while rattletrap trucks of her neighbors
wheeze their lonely ways home.
The customer counts out a little more time
and speaks to his hands of love.
They wrinkle like nuns around his white cup.

The schizophrenic night imagines clouds
and cries on the cheeks of the carver.
She listens for some alien whisper of love
and the ragged wings of *empty* sigh across the room.

A heavy batter of dreams flutters under her ribs.
We are mute testimony to a lusterless magic.

The joys of love.
Next time, next time let's speak of dreams.

AUTUMN

We are not our own light. –Malebranche

Evening chill yellows the apple,
plum leaves redden and sleepy lovers
curl against one another, settling down.

Nasturtiums hold their orange babushkas
to the breast of a scrawny fog.

First stars gleam sudden as a thrill,
the moon a stiff wave from an absentee sun.

Now the earth, dark as a lover's eyes,
whispers that old promise of a last long hug before light.

VESPERS

Mother church clings to you like incense.
Hear the censer's *click   click   click*
against the Bishop's ring?
Rings, our holy penance, ghost my dreams.

Timid as Trappists, lonely mendicants, we whisper
Love, a breathless confession, across the line.
I remember you had first-communion eyes.

THE TERMITES WING INTO SUNSET

Nighthawks fatten themselves in long, daring dives.
Soon, the bats.

Say an old couple grew up out here.
Some August he might call to her:

Look, honey, flying ants. She'd glance up, then
back to those ancient flutterings, her hands.

Outside the window, two plump-bellied hatchlings claim a stump
drop their flimsy wings and begin their long, ritual dance.

FISH CAMP AT LAPUSH

Love is never finished expressing itself. –Gaston Bachelard

We scoop a hollow in this sandy bed
and ride the tender currents of our mattress.
Mold sprawls the walls like seaweed behind your candle.
Our sudden cries, night gulls on the wind.

Fishermen next door snore off whisky
their wives scuff to the bathroom, back.
Like salmon, they sniff out streams
and drag their wasting bodies after.

We wriggle against our own salt sea
scaleless flanks thrash the moonlight.
Fishermen groan themselves awake.
These supple skins we slap together could be waves.

BURNING CATERPILLARS

First, cut the whole branch off clean at the trunk.
Their black heads bend and rebend
singing the thrum of your thickening heart.

Dopple the kerosene over their backs
and those jewels on their shoulders blink open:
a string of wide, bronze eyes.

Your daughter, who's crying, speak to her. Turn,
strike the match, step back and their thousand hissing souls
scream *beauty beauty* high and thin in this pining wind.

THE PLACE

That cold damp breast of death settles over you,
and the must of her moldy down stoppers your lungs
clutch her so close she shrieks her way off,
your hot breath filling her claw.

Then get out, live that one good dream you've hidden
somewhere between your eyes and the bottom of your pillow.
The night has nothing to do with this.
Hitchhike. Beg. You know.

Feel your center lift out of you
billow out into the day, a long, easy sigh.
This time her breast is warm, and the sweet smell of her
fills you up, up to her, and gone.

Orientation 4.

Always carry cigars and a light, they cut the stink.

MORNING FERRY TO THE WORLD

Porpoises weave tongues of daybreak and the foaming Strait down
their supple backs. What meaning behind their smiles?

Our ferry muscles away miles, fog and this inevitable,
indomitable tide that laps at light and dark and the shadow between.

Pacing the decks without you, I'm only
half-full of wonder, only halfway breathless.

EVENING RAIN

Thunder dodges the scorching day until evening,
when wind whips real rain across our valley, swelling
our parched little stream into mountain flood.
We wake to a bit of reality when someone yells
on some winding path, indistinctly and faintly,
while somewhere else, exposed to the sun for three days
the spikes of thatch grass, ready to be brooms, are lost.

No one really exists nearby at that moment,
onset of this rain seems simply
to drive a chickadee early to its nest.
Some kind of darkness drives the flood because
the rain still thunders outside, a blurred, realistic wail.
Yes, we thought the rain would never fall,
our people would never have accidents,
and those white stones, they would forever
refuse doom. In the murmuring sound of their prayers
we find ourselves to be just some objects–now near, now far:
We used to be so primitive, so easily startled.

> –Lü De'an
> Trans. by Ying Qin and Bill Ransom

CHECK-UP

How long do I have to wait here?
Write a poem,
lighten these heavy prognostications.

The bee needle stabs a vein
"buzz" lights up the heart
(radiation isn't related to emotion, generally speaking).
Seductive green snake curves across the monitor.
Want to eat the forbidden fruit?
Curve up? Yang and strength: bird's dancing wings.
Curve down? Accept the bleeding.
To relax is no sign of giving up.
In a *snap* it swirls away, sheds skin,
apple peels everywhere.

Outside the windowblind, youths
surround a brand new Volkswagen,
take turns in the driver's seat, touch here, there.
Have you touched the tail? Where is it hidden?
An apple tree buds out. Bees swarm.

Speed up. He extends one finger.
Steps quicken, have to run. Climb.
At first, morning always filled us with
confidence, how beautiful,
how strong! Watch them shoulder to shoulder
sharing a cigarette, so cool, kiss each other's
lip petals or fuzzy cheeks.
Speed up. Two fingers now,
heart beats, blue fork tongue licks, contracts
the red light,
still ten more seconds.

Enter the cold machine, white metal arms
curve, hold me tight, hands behind my head
expose both armpits, like when I was young
without warning or wariness

(Mom!)
heart suddenly
loud
Mom singing, my cries, and
the pink fluorescent dye
symbolizes blood (or rubies)
shines on the branches of flowering
youth, his garden. Even if
surrounded by gold, I still
see the innocent glimmer
contracting ahead,
forty years of age
can I expect
more?

We will see each other again, youngster
believe or not
you turn and don't look at me, blow a smoke ring
swaying, divergent, not a blink, so what?
They don't go home,
Star light, star bright.

Tomorrow the results from life.
These kids will take the world for a spin
everything is normal, everything's all right.
Narrowing those eyes without eyelids,
snake, so flamboyant
scribbles out its secrets to no one.

–Zhang Er
Trans. by the poet and Bill Ransom

SCENERY

After many years of disappointment,
I finally removed the window,
but after a second thought, actually
what I took along was just its frame.

Well-bottom dark, the world is still
where it is after I turn away
to walk in its distant places,
treasuring this window frame.

Those familiar migratory birds fly the edge of the sky.
Imagine that I was all the same then,
walking repeatedly past this or that remote place,
carrying my particular scenery on my back.

> –Lü De'an
> Trans. by Ying Qin & Bill Ransom

GRASS SPROUTING

can't crawl out
these grass roots peed on by dogs or human,
tree, pigeons work their wings to take off
bottom of the pot, beside the crib
watch that grass greening outside the window
the child naps, curled and content
the house is clean.

can't crawl upward to
the flow of light and wind
Get close, closer, see clearly the grass blade
fluffy with life echo
that still river from afar
kind of. Let it be.
Lie down just like this, to leave
so why is it not good? Pretty
you are already beauty:
high perch, next to water, flowers and trees
and white stone fences.
Remember reality!
house chores, office, child learning to talk
husband restless.

Farewell dinner, farewell drink, one last hour
measures all, decorates this backyard
remember everything, care about everything
and hear that train rushing off
catch the one hour banquet of the morning glory
leave, leaving
delighted heart, light eternal.

–Zhang Er
Trans. by the poet and Bill Ransom

AFTER WORK

On the street, traffic thickens,
people jostle backpacked shoulders
bags clutched to chests, handles in hands, arms in arms.
Dogs. Neighbors return, keys click in doors.
Joggers sweat in their long shorts,
waddle past the doorway.

Life sparks anew, peaceful faces smiling and polite
frying food smells, young deliveryman.
TV stir-fries today's events
sets them on the table. The sun punches out,
children school up, cry, laugh.
Trees and their beloved shadows entwine as
dreams become true, after work.

> –Zhang Er
> Trans. by the poet and Bill Ransom

THE HEAVIEST THING

–for Malan

Dig out the heaviest thing
stuff it into your mouth, drink down
desire, drifting from left atrium to the right atrium:
one hand can't comprehend the other hand's
stony, sorrowful heart. Emotion? Slide
under the bottom of your log boat, carve out
this stark unforgetting water.

Rain sweeps into the dark. Heavy
is neither the stories you write nor
your voice over the sea. Depression
in fact is very light, whatever can be said
is light. As light as that rainbow
on an Andes mountain, breathless, between your fingers
trickling down from the blue air–
you throw yourself into the sun right in front of me.

Let them climb up and down these boulders
you polished so smooth and gentle:
still, if they want elevation they surrender
the squeeze near your navel, pile up
pile upward these structures of worship. You and they
body-limb enlaced!
Bodies and limbs inlaid like stones of a wall, concepts-locked
sentences wind-tight cocoon the heroine of your stories.

The highest banner above the heads is
not necessarily the heaviest.
He says your conclusion is fake. I say the stories
must be true then. "So boring," you laugh.
You hang your *ha!ha!ha!* around the corner of your mouth.
Laugh louder and be saved!
But they insist on the mask, the anesthesia,
you grab a pen
you count: one, two, three…
"Hey!"—

bloom open a pond of lotus: Lotus Girl
  two fingers pinch her red paper
    limpid water, a flirtatious light.

              –Zhang Er
              Trans. by the poet and Bill Ransom

ROSE HIPS

–for Camille

Elegant eyebrows pick up the shadow of things
well balanced flavor: sweet and sour. The tea cup, Japanese,
the tea and saucer, English. Country music anthems
normal life in the fifties way, rightfully assured.
Does this winter morning sunlight warm your desk as well?
Separated by one river, a few blocks, desks
shoulder to shoulder almost a mirror. You do up your hair
to elongate your neck, expose collarbones, seem slimmer
for whom? What else can we discuss besides
boyfriends of different races, a daughter of mixed blood?
These things so close to flesh do not leave shadow, yet firmly
block our vision, as the needle of light trapped in
the soundtrack of time, repeating that nonsensical note
                    Eng Eng Eng Eng

Sprinkle on some pepper, and sugar, an appetite uneasy,
tender eggs and bread fresh from the oven. What to serve first?
The waiter frowns. Desire barks on the street corner, then
flees ahead of the police siren. Where does the horse run? Does it matter?
You want to wait to learn to ride until the spring warm days:
boots and hard hat, breeches and flowery scarf through
wild flowers over the hill. I say freedom is only an
imagination as this tight-fit outfit perfectly
proves. Better not to catch the fantasy
for who can escape the shadow between our legs?
So we're pulled, dragged down desperate, table base
dark and heavy. Iron. Under the rose, a hip.

How to exorcise the doomsday horror
of that giant garland on the window:
stuck on a single syllable doesn't allow us to be slender forever, forever
smiling without shadow. The tea cup and saucer near your hand define
the reality of order and the necessity of the weightlessness.

Difficult situation: live too long, feel too little.
Difficult situation: live too short, feel too much.

Yes, we are conflicted, unresolved, unable to escape,
like sunlight moves from my desk to yours,
bright yet on the thick leaves of the tulip cast the broken shadows of
petals. Flower vase stands freely, separated from the sugar jar
by an uncrossable distance. We can't handle things
in front of our eyes, arriving too early or coming too late
though we only want to live in the present, only at this
moment while there are yet shadows.

Let's just write, in Chinese or English, use vocabulary
in rhyme with life. Those things that lost their shine
do not lose their shadows.
Only after the bloom, come the tasty hips
suffusing pink memories from the bottom of the cup.
Isn't it from the bubbly emotion
steam rises? We can, with our accent, speak clearly
if only of our problems. Repeat, if we must
repeat. Forget the helpless frivolousness at hand.
Maybe only by living through memory
the sentence can steady its soles
    in the melancholy soil
        under our desks.

                    –Zhang Er
                    Trans. by the poet and Bill Ransom

DEEP NIGHT

Deep in the night, I dream of you overlooking the depths
from the heights. Above the ocean, a seabird swoops low,
tall, tall buildings crowd both shores.
You wave toward the bird,
as if letting it know that you are here: where?
We used to sleep on the 18th floor. The sea shrinks now
in your pupil. That bird flies, like a panorama of a bird.
I feel your loneliness, hold you tight,
feel the fainting heaviness of your soft body
falling, falling, when looking a bird's-eye view,
however, this last fall is inside my body.
We make love, that is also my wanting to let you know,
I am here, the continued flight of the bird
is nothing but its taking a fly before sleep.
Maybe it wants, with the help of the light from our room,
to follow those dark shoals of fish, while on the surface
our light flickers, all the way through, to the bottom of the sea.

–Lü De'an
Trans. by Ying Qin & Bill Ransom

eMAIL

Not much to be discussed further
is there, Father?
Those long grasses spill over the hill, blooms blacken
in shadow as sunlight measures out square by square
the city at attention, in time to me, too,
a patch of screen grayish white—
anything more to chat?
Whatever wants to be said loses
its voice and body.
Silence.

are you home?
Home, or hiking high mountains far away. A dog
snuffles around under the bench then
shuffles off. A sparrow tempted to jump to a shoulder,
yet no. At that moment I feel the real loss:
good-bye, it is getting late
Darkness and a warm afterglow
close over the screen.

> –Zhang Er
> Trans. by the poet and Bill Ransom

LOST LOVERS

All life's losses gather
into this tree, and why not?
This nesting and rest stop for so many birds
blooms and sheds in front of my window.
Dogs in heat stroll by, pee,
and children score their goals here.

There must be a place, some star-stunned sliver of sky
for old loves to gather, staring from afar
pretending dispassion, maybe strolling over
under disguise to ask for a light, knowing
that the old beanstalk has long burnt to ash. Dreams
may still kiss the forehead, play out a dramatic
adventure (you again glide in the glittering lake
and can't swim out), or bid you to count out
a measure of brittle leaves. Falling,
unaware, you all fall down,
beanpods pop in my hands. Dearest,
this compost heap of losses becomes me
awake, facing this unsayable

blank page.

> –Zhang Er
> Trans. by the poet & Bill Ransom

SILHOUETTES

Father and I
saunter side by side.
The autumn rain hesitates
in this cavernous lull after
the last outburst of rain.

We amble the intervals
between rain and rain
shoulder to shoulder, distinct
clear, not a word to say.

We just walked out from the house
so there's not a word left to say
after our long life together.
Water drops like the snap
of a brittle willow twig.

Like plum blossoms through winter
father's hair is already all white
halo of a kind soul, respectable.

Still this is the familiar street
all familiar people should wave their regards
father and I both walk peacefully
in an unutterable loving-kindness.

–Lü De'an
Trans. by Ying Qin & Bill Ransom

ORIENTATION

You'll know if you're made for this when you
bag your first body part. A leg by itself is
heavier than you'd think. Dead babies,
no matter what killed them, wake you
for the rest of your nights. Always carry
cigars and a light, they cut the stink.
Maggots won't hurt you, but they mean:
Handle with care; things come apart.
Remember, all bleeding stops.

WHERE THE WORD FOR WAIT IS HOPE

Sunset bloodies every face it touches.
Lovers stroll their secrets, soldiers
roll their tongues across unkissed lips
and stroke their short automatics.

Weight shifts, shadows pool in the street,
safeties click to the rhythm of a daydream,
to the sway of tight northamerican jeans.
A blind drummer chainsmokes Winstons at the bar.

From the alley-mouths come the sucking sounds
of time at the breast, of dark history
swallowing somebody whole. Bloody snouts
root barbed wire and glass.

Love survives in soft tongues and whispers.
Life depends on signs: two rocks pinning a red bandanna,
a branch across the road, the right word.
Geography here reflects politics and the wind.

That one-armed lottery vendor's fingers
fold and re-fold somebody's chances.
Tonight jaguars and monkeys run the streets,
the moon itself a million-caliber scar.

PETÉN

*What can you do when you have hunger all the time
and the bugs won't let you sleep?* –guatemalteca

Soldiers disperse for the night in their grim
tight patrols. The Maya woman tending bar
smiles them a thin-lipped smile. "No me gustan,"
she whispers. "They don't please me."

They shoot monkeys in the bush, save the rum
for themselves. They quit shooting buzzards
when the dead just stank longer.
A stutter of unsteady fire signals "Last Call."

Listen here to the warble of night-toads
down by the lake. Smell the sweet bloom
of White Nuns lining the roadside.
Like us, this country was made for love.

BOMBEROS VOLUNTARIOS: GUATEMALA

Firefighting is our common language here:
take away air, fuel, or heat and you win,
whether in Guatemala or Gig Harbor.

Firefighting in Guatemala means picking up
the morning dead. Means not talking to reporters,
to family, not even to each other about guts
spread across the road, lips carved into a smile,

hands in pockets with both arms missing.
Always the daily paperwork, even down here.
We save ink, ourselves, our precious time:
"Exposure," "Machete accident," "Natural causes."

FLIES

for Tom Jay
I heard a fly buzz when I died. –Emily Dickinson

From our high ladders in spring we
ripped boards off the old farmhouse wall
and dreamed our plans for your new barn.
Crowbars snapped a century of dust
into hair, nose, lung. We tasted
death, birth, celebration, sorrow.

Our third course of prying liberated the flies.
Like sizzling, crawling dust they
infested our noses and our mouths, clung
by thousands to our hair and faces, they
scrabbled down shirt collars, up our
sleeves and pants legs where we

slapped and scooped and cringed against the
scratchings of a swarm of legs, the
crisp tickle of those frantic wings.
One-handed on ladder-tops, we fought
this curse, tucked our shirts over our mouths,
breathed deep and kept on working.

We wanted that wood. No one would salvage
for us. Rich in friendship, wallets empty,
we shuddered on into the filthy days.
Now I train guerrillas in rescue, and
green meat stinks the roadside grass:
somebody's son, brother, husband.

His penis rots in a slack, speechless mouth.
Two men vomit; one swats at flies,
coughs, contemplates the smoky horizon.
How these maggots, those sons and daughters
of that ludicrous marriage of flies, love us!
His split, swollen belly buzzes and whispers

in this egg-laying frenzy. He shimmers
with sunlight off a blanket of busy wings.
His family wants him. We lift, and
his legs slip out of his pants, these
two purple clubs a last joke from the death squad.
Empty pants legs flap the blistering breeze

and still ripple through my restless dreams.
I hate some men, a few pernicious women,
and all those persistent, ubiquitous flies.

MARKET DAY

Your driver picks up the government guide at the village gate.
Young and jittery, this fast-talking boy gets on your nerves that
heat already baked raw. You offer money for silence, which
he takes, and more to drive where you want, which he refuses.
Never has anyone here refused your money. Your driver lifts
an eyebrow, winks at you in his mirror. You've heard stories
of prisoners here, a massacre, another to come. Your driver
knows the place and your guide is the army's guarantee that you
won't find it. This narrow street splits at a wall, your driver
cranks the wheel hard right, your guide pounds the dashboard
And shouts, "¡Alto! ¡Alto! ¡Alto!" Spittle flecks the windshield
and there, past the roadblock, you see razor wire and women
fenced like cattle in a field. You click off a few pictures,
your driver burns rubber in reverse. He winks again in the mirror,
takes a left while your guide swears eloquently for his age. There,
a block ahead, you see the park and the weekly market. The guide
runs off, and before the army can hunt you down, you buy yourself
and your driver a beer and a shirt and you get the hell out of town.

NEBAJ

In this photo you see the village backed up
against a lush green hill. Paths between those
pole-and-thatch homes shine from the steady
shuffle of bare feet burdened with firewood,
charcoal, water and cotton. Look here

at the heaped-up dirt that could be a fence
that walls in the village. See the ditch behind?
You might think runoff, irrigation, a feudal
protection against attack. This silent village
holds its breath, you have to be there to feel it.

Flashes of blue and red behind those pole walls
are women. Wide dark eyes look out for their men,
for those lucky few who ran when the army came.
If you look carefully at the corners of the ditches
you see two machine guns aimed right at you.

Your army has not yet killed your sons, and so
far it hasn't thought to hold your women hostage.
Those hard-eyed men behind the guns have water,
food, patience and ammunition. Men always
come back for their women. Wouldn't you?

PHOTO OF THE GALERÍA

Burlap sacks hang like old cocoons from pole rafters,
each one a family's treasures. The army burned the rest.
Three hundred women take turns standing. Others sit, nap,
nurse the surviving children. The men are dead. No one
cries. An armed guard escorts them one by one to humiliation
at the open latrine. One by one to the water source, one by one
to their single tortilla and tablespoon of beans each day. Their
bright red skirts, their white blouses embroidered with reds, blues,
greens and yellows represent the lives they cashed in simply
for being Indios. Every pitiful plot of holy corn and scrawny beans
means one less coffee plant sending lattes to Seattle.
They all know the color of coffee here. The color of their eyes.
The color of sun-baked blood.

CATEQUISTA

Village faithful lay down fresh petals in red and white
Mayan geometrics from airport to national cathedral.
Tomorrow the Pope will kiss this grieving earth and
crush these petals under his new bulletproof tires.

Soldiers fidget at the ready while a giant cross
tilts into place at the end of this fragrant path.
Their gazes flick about the crowd, and their
fingers click *select* to *full auto* on their rifles.

Religion is dangerous business here. The president
preaches in tongues and offers real blood to the highlands.
This woman beside me stinks. She walked barefoot
three hundred miles for a glimpse of the car of the Pope.

Her foot, black with gangrene, split like a ripe plum,
oozes something thick and green onto these crisp,
white petals. "Help me," she whispers, "in the name
of God." She will die here, and soon, with or without God.

But I spend a handful of Ceclor on my conscience,
tell her the foot has to come off, point her to the clinic.
She nods. Her lusterless eyes stare at hope in her palm.
I shift my aging sack of healthy flesh upwind.

DESCONOCIDO

The Canadian and I practiced that drill
over and over. Three armed men:
Come with us. Get in the van.
To get in the van is to die in pieces.

Don't speak Spanish, spread hands
wide, act confused. Make them
come. Best if they poke your chest
with the muzzle. A pistol? Grab
the muzzle, shove, twist and snatch.

Kick his crotch, grab his hair and
shoot the man behind. Shoot the
next. A rifle? Even simpler.
Many hundred times I practiced that
grab and never a hammer dropped.

Take it in the hand, give it in the head,
you said. We choreographed life's greatest joke.

Twice a week I make that move in dreams,
drink too much, pity my naïve countrymen.
I have these few regrets: time and
money wasted, good women ignored
and your real name I can't recall.

GLIMPSE OF THE DEATH SQUAD

The Maya woman in the bright red collar
sells melon slices in the doorway shade.
She flicks flies from the lips of her daughter
curled on the rag at our feet.

Two men in gray suits lean in the sun
against the open doors of their brown Ford Bronco.
Their mirror sunglasses reflect four northamericans
glancing up from four tiny Maya women.

The warm watermelon drips on the blanket.
I hold it away from my shirt, step to the curb
and both men stiffen. One unbuttons his jacket,
reaches inside smooth as a magician, a gambler.

On the front seat: a clipboard, a walkie-talkie,
and a new Uzi submachine gun, folded like a bud.
On the clipboard: three names, too small to read.
The four tiny Americans take four red bites of melon.

We smile at the driver, toast him with the rind.
He nods. Those Maya women in his sunglasses
never look up. The windows in the Bronco are black.
I've never tasted a fruit so juicy, so sweet.

THE BABY IN THE BASKET

Lies atop a hard bed of grenades and under
the red blanket her grandmother wove. Her
mother steps carefully over one body, over
the next, whispers *Diós, ayúdanos* instead of
making the sign of the cross, the basket and her
mission too heavy for that. Across the smoky street,
Don Luis unlocks the gate to his funeral parlor,
the glitter of opportunity lights his eyes. She
sets her basket on the step of blue door #5, lifts
the baby, leaves the blanket, hurries home, her
basket warm and brown eggs ready to hatch.

SUNRISE GRENADE

In the hole in the shooting I crouch against a green Datsun, fender
rotted through, and hug my medical kit to my chest. The soldier
on the other side *snicks* a new magazine and jacks in a round.
Hope makes a move for the hotel doorway that my body won't follow.

How to describe that *click-click-click*ing I'll never forget?
A goat in tap shoes skipping down the street? The future?

A *slap* of fire smacks my shins, and I drop.
The soldier faces God and leaks under the Datsun.
I jump for the doorway, fall and scramble, my bag crooked
in my arm like a football. My hearing comes back almost perfect.

Over "I love Lucy" in Spanish, I pick Guatemala out of my shins.
Lucy, she's got some 'splainin' to do.

Orientation 5.

Maggots won't hurt you, but they mean:
Handle with care; things come apart.

YOLANDA

Something empty nagged at my life, you know?
Servants for the house, driver for the cars, gardeners,
nannies, security guards and razor fence. Sit home,
smoke, talk to my plants. My husband had his work,
his travel, his women's scents drenching his shorts.

Oh, yes, the plantation wives gossiped at noon, nattered
of meals they couldn't cook, embassy parties and those blonde
northamerican snobs. One languid morning, between sweet
rolls and trivia, a bare stick of a man slipped security
and shoved his filthy rag of a baby into my arms.

"Doctor," he gasped. "In the name of God." In the lap
of my best housedress, on the leather seat of my Mercedes,
right in front of the Archbishop's cathedral, she died. The
doctor tossed her into the furnace and never asked her name.
The father? One of our coffee pickers; he disappeared.

His insolence and our security killed him, I know that now. So,
my driver took me back to the cathedral, and I asked Monsignor
"What can I do?" I bought him the transmitter that got him
killed, divorced my husband, learned to cook, to drive, to shoot,
learned to love my daughters more than gold. Yes, we won.

What you heard is true: my signature dries on the UN papers.
Black as ink, it is the blood of that baby, of Monsignor Romero,
of Roque Dalton and the priests and nuns and those unclaimed bones
at El Playón. Better to die in rags than to kill in silks.

LOVE AND WAR, SALVADORAN STYLE

The comandantes meet in the kitchen, their table
a litter of ashtrays and maps. Boiled coffee sours
on the burner. Your new husband bats tennis balls
a lifetime to the north, and we take your honeymoon here.

We squeeze together on a child's single bed, Neruda
at our heads and Lorca at our feet. Lorca, in a Russian/
Spanish edition, hasn't yet mapped the terrain of betrayal
that will execute him. Altitude reminds us we're dying,

too, one gasp at a time, one spasm at a time, a string
of little deaths wedding us to this war for eternity.

THE DWARF

Every day I saw his bright blue eyes and the flash of his white teeth when the bottle came up. He never took a drink while I passed, only held the bottle quivering at the pink droop of his lower lip. The dwarf never scared me like those other men on Camilla Street, but I skirted his stoop every day just the same. I would have asked him some things, but Martita says that only whores speak to men first. So, it's true that he never spoke to me. His big face and burly, stubby arms were nearly black because he sat outside all day. When he drank under the midday sun, the dwarf's blue eyes glittered like opals. All I knew for sure: he was a blue-eyed dwarf who sat on his stoop and drank. I walked past him twice a day on my way to the market on Boulevard Venezuela, and I never knew his name.

He came here after the cease-fire, like those others, Chele and Monk. Those two like to say things to me, things that a man should not say to a woman. Some days they sprawl right in the path and I have to jump the ditch and walk in the sun. Just yesterday I walked the ditchside in the hot sun to stay away from them because Monk was relieving himself while Chele called to me, *Look, Beautiful, at the man of this man!* But the dwarf, everyone called him "the dwarf" or "the blue-eyes," he never bothered me. The dwarf never grunted at me or whispered or made the little sucking noises with his lips. He never stood in my way on my path to the market, like Chele and Monk, and he never tried to trap me against the wall. True, he never moved to save me, either. But save me for what? I know, now, something of his despair.

Martita told me only yesterday that every dwarf is a wizard and blue eyes are trouble, and anyone on Camilla Street will tell you that Martita is as wise a woman as she is rich. I have my own plan to get rich. Here in the city, working in the guesthouse, I spend nothing and save everything. Martita says that's how she started, but I know that a loan from her mother helped her out. My mother was killed in that incident at the river.

Something to drink, please. Water, yes, thanks.

The dwarf won't look at you, Martita said, and crossed herself. *That means he's seen your soul.*

Someone who is not God has seen my soul!

Everything, Martita whispered. She crossed herself again and spit at the rooster. *He sees everything!*

Chele and Monk are drunks, as the dwarf was a drunk, and perhaps if they could have seen into my soul they would have left me alone, too. I have not forgotten how to do what I did at the river. The other men here, they are good men, they watch out for me. They laugh at Chele when Chele whispers to me in his man-voice, Beauty, Beauty. With the good men around, sitting on their steps, Chele never touches me. That Monk, he doesn't care who sees, he is a bad one for the touching. So the dwarf never looked up when I passed, but now I know he knew the other good men were there to help me. Something happened to him in the war, just as something happened to me at the river, and that's what he stares at so hard when he drinks. When he drank.

Every day for two months I saw his bright blue eyes, yes, and the flash of his white teeth when the bottle came up. Always he looked somewhere else—at his small, twisted feet or at the ants on the path. His stubby hands like a baby's tipped the bottle back but he never took a drink while I passed, though sometimes he held the little bottle quivering at his lips. Nothing. Other men on Camellia Street were drunk by midday, but the dwarf was the only drunk who never scared me.

When I hurried by Chele and Monk this morning, I saw the dwarf stretched out across the path, an empty Toro Rojo bottle under his left foot. I stepped over his crossed feet and felt that empty-stomach feeling I get when the Santa Tecla bus goes too fast downhill. He faced away from me, towards his open door, and I heard that Cuban, Silvio Rodriguez, singing from a tape machine inside. I had a cousin in the mountains who was shot by the army for having a Silvio Rodriguez tape, so it couldn't be the radio. The dwarf's music blared from beside his open door, and a woman yelled something I couldn't understand from the back of his house. I thought at first that she was part of the music until I glanced up and saw her standing back there in the dark, naked. She had the whitest skin I have ever seen, and thick red hair past her shoulders. She lifted her chin and shouted something at me, in English, I think, and she laughed. I was embarrassed and hurried up to Boulevard Venezuela. Martita needed the bags for the vacuum cleaner before the new guests came, so until I returned from the market I didn't know for sure he was dead.

I didn't want to risk my soul and step over him again, and the ditch on the other side of the path is wide and filthy, so I stepped up onto his stoop to get around. No blood, and I didn't touch him, but I knew by the emptiness around me that he was dead—like someone stole the cross from the roof of the church and put a picture of a cross in its place. I looked back, towards the market, and two soldiers from the garrison rounded the corner. I stepped into the doorway. "Señora!" I called. "Señora!" No one answered. This time I heard the radio, an announcement from the government about turning in weapons. I was not afraid to be there alone with him, but I was afraid of the soldiers so I turned to the dwarf again, and this time I saw his eyes. His head rested on his right hand and faced the doorway, and his blue eyes looked past me into a greater mystery than his tidy kitchen or my pitiful soul. A trail of small black ants explored his slightly blue, slightly open lips. I hurried to the corner at Avenida Los Abetos before I looked back. The two soldiers almost passed the dwarf, but then the younger one must have felt the emptiness, too. He nudged the dwarf with his boot, nudged again. Then he shrugged to his partner. They looked both ways, up and down the street. Chele and Monk and the rest of the men had disappeared as soon as the soldiers first rounded the corner, so the street was as quiet as the breath not taken. I could tell what they were thinking, that this dead dwarf was a lot of trouble. They shrugged again and, after only a glance into his doorway, they continued their patrol, and I hurried down Los Abetos to get the bags to Martita before her guests arrived.

NICARAGUA

That first afternoon in the village they bring me the boy
shot by a Contra while hoeing beans. Bones click
in his thin neck cradled in the bloody arms of his father. His
mother kneels and weeps, a quick afternoon rain patters
as the parrots swoop in, my hands and my heart
as empty now as the vision in the boy's black eyes.

My hands and the bullet are Americans. The hoe, East
German, the day, fragrant and unforgiving as God. The
father lays his son at my feet. A last bubble of blood bursts
from his lips and I remember my daughter, her bubblegum
and how much I love her. "Save him," the father whispers.
"Through God, save my son." I can't even save myself.

My stethoscope silences the crowd. I hear its feathery rasp
on skin, the chatter of parrots, the plop-plop of my sweat
against his skinny chest. His pupils, like the rest of us,
like the sun and the rain and the afternoon parrots, are fixed.
I can't look up, I can't stand; I want to run and weep and
shoot that sniper who is just someone else's son trying to come home.

EXPATRIATES

Our dirt-floor Managua office housed Somoza's National Guard.
A mango's throw from the Intercontinental, we collar arms dealers,
politicians and ex-CIA here to swill a poor man's last warm beer.

Jorge sweeps up an M-16 magazine, like those agents,
loaded and corroded. Underneath, half a pair of handcuffs and
a handful of pearls from somebody's brother's smile.

The three Salvadorans ignore the teeth, race against
the afternoon power failure and tap tactics into three
stripped-down laptops. That fax-modem on the one
line out, now *there's* a mouth with fine, sharp teeth.
There's a mouth with a bite left to it.

SLEIGHT OF HAND

Nothing in Managua is what it seems.
A magic geology turns buildings back to stones,
students wave the stones and a dictator disappears.
The dead, the roads and the treasury vanish with him.
Quick-fingered children appear in their place,
a lifetime of hunger hides up their sleeves.

An address here is the second blue door past
the church towards the mountain in this, the
capital city of the country that my president fears.
Glare simmers fatigue, vision wavers under shade
of my hand. Over there, a dozen old men sit
still as stone in a dozen doorways.

A girl walks by, a spill of coins scatters at her feet.
One old man kneels to gather them up, and he has
no hands. She scoops his coins into his pouch, smiles,
waves goodbye. Those old men wave back, and not one
of them has hands. Somewhere a great basket of hands
fingers a poor country's treasury, counting its incredible cost.

DOBLE TRACCIÓN

Sunday afternoon, we're in the old Lada, Adán's driving.
I squeeze in back with the kids. We're heading for an ex-dictator's
private lake for a dip. I need to say "four-wheel drive"
for tomorrow to get in and out of the mountains.
My pocket dictionary reveals what I already know:
"four" and "wheel" and "to drive." Yolanda glances me
that look she gave when I announced I was pregnant and
meant embarrassed. "A truck that drives with all wheels
of force." Everyone laughs. "Claro," Yolanda says.
"Es 'doble tracción.'" The kids test my pronunciation.
Test again. Then, talk about borrowing a doble tracción
for tomorrow. We'll lie—the roads up north are mined,
and good trucks, hard to come by. We pass an old man driving
a mule cart full of shell casings. "¡Mira, Bill!" Angelina
leans across me to point at the mule: "¡Doble tracción!"

THUNDER

We call that border artillery thunder
and this vast, deserted beach our own.
One grizzled fisherman brings turtle eggs
says we're the first to come this far
since what we call thunder moved in
a couple of kilometers north. The lime

is free. Across the bay El Salvador glowers
at you, its conscience, and at me, your extra hands.

Stones in the surf urge our feet, *Move on!*
We pack up our gear and prepare our hike to the thunder.
You gaze, weeping, across that forbidden bay:
"We could walk to your home or mine on this same beach."
From Southern Cross to Big Dipper, we're one family
sharing food on a single beach that we all call home.

FANCY FOOTWORK

The afternoon rush of parrots through Ceibas reminds us that there is
no twilight here. Dusk lasts only moments, then the nightsong and the
Contra sweep the thick, sweating dark. At this crossroads, in our old
Toyota, we wait. That Datsun ahead and the Lada behind, they wait,
too. In the Datsun, two young men from the literacy program. They
teach woodcutters and chicle-hunters how to puzzle out those marks on
paper that let so many foreigners own their lives. The young men share
a lunch of cold black beans. In the Lada, four French who painted our
clinic tire of taking pictures and sing political songs. Then they snap
at each other and snooze. The Contra mined the only road home, and
we wait to see who will go first. At dark, we'll be ambushed. Even with
these bunions, my feet are happy where they are. They itch and tingle
in their muddy shoes, and they wait, and in their waiting hope the army
will send a truck back south. They pray it's heavy, with a narrow track.
They know better than to pray for no mines. Did I tell you about the
records these feet set in track? The temptations they've led me into?
I should've danced when I had the chance. Headlights bounce in the
rear-view mirror. An army truck roars past, honking, the soldiers wave
us on. I drive right in their track, and we're gossiping again when a
white flash rolls the truck, and we stop. Cuts, a broken collarbone, two
skinny legs nearly gone at the shins. We load them all up, creep onward
to town. After the hospital,

we look for some music,

and we dance.

BOILOVER

Due south off the Honduran border, shadows take
the road, twilight just a wink in God's eye. The Contra
slither through rising chitters and rustles and night-warbles.
Headlights are targets here, and the mines, invisible.
Water gauge points red, steam haloes our hood in that fat
rising moon. A jeep skids into our bumper. "Let's go!"
Two young Sandinistas wave us on, gray-skinned
in the moonlight, luminous hair: "We cleared those mines already!"
We all scan the roadsides. I point out the steam:
"We need water." A lieutenant my daughter's age
taps the roof. "Follow us." We can't follow him.
A mutter, movement in the shadows. Scrape of metal
against rock. The driver fills his mess kit from his radiator,
sloshes it into ours. Again. *Hurry!* And three more times
Hurry! Hurry! Hurry! Again. *Tap-tap* on the roof:
"Follow us. Water ahead—leave devil Contra the night."

PASSING THE WATER TRUCK

I'm driving a truckload of Salvadorans south into Managua. Toyota crew-cab long-bed four-wheel-drive five-speed diesel. We can't get these in my country at any price. It lives to spite war and the worst roads in the world. Dirt and fatigue stoke our sweaty silence. We reach the pavement marking the long climb before our drop into sanctuary.

"I can smell the lake already," Yolanda says.

We're tailing the bumper of a full water truck wallowing away our patience at seven kilometers an hour. The sign at the roadside says, "No Passing." The water truck driver grinds into granny, and I imagine a hundred tons of water crushing us all against the bank of the curve. That string of cars behind us honks its opinion. The Salvadorans grumble. I pass.

Cheers from the Salvadorans and the cars behind. The water truck driver blasts a warning, shakes a scolding finger at me as a young Sandinista soldier steps from the leafy shade into my lane. His bright orange gloves wave us to a stop. The Salvadorans and I scramble for our papers. I spread mine across my lap.

"Don't worry, Nicaragua is different," Yolanda says. "Relax, this isn't Salvador." The Salvadorans don't buy it, and neither do I.

"No matter," I say. "Anywhere in the world, soldiers are trouble."

She lifts an eyebrow, and I see the upturned palm at my window.

"License, please," he says. "Anywhere in the world, careless drivers are trouble." The water truck driver waves as he passes, and I hand over my Washington State Driver's License. All he sees is "WASHINGTON."

He tips the bill of his cap back, looks me in the eye and asks, "Do you know Jorge Bush? Do you know the man who brings this war to us?"

I don't, and I explain about the state being different from the capital. He's sweating, we're all sweating. A tentative honk from down the line breaks the quiet.

"The sign says 'No Passing,'" he says. "You passed."

I start about the clear road ahead, about getting to Managua before dark, and he puts a finger to his lips.

"The sign says 'No Passing,'" he repeats. "You passed."

Yolanda pokes me.

"Yes," I admit, "I passed."

"Someone passed here yesterday," he says, "and four people died. The colonel sent me here for a month to stop people from passing. You see how hot it can be. You see the dirt. You have your friends with you, I have no one. For a month. Because someone passed, and the sign said 'No Passing.'"

He hands back my license, and Yolanda pours him a cup of water. He thanks her, drinks half. She nods, he downs the rest.

"Now," he says, "when you see a sign that says 'No Passing,' will you pass?"

"Absolutely not," I say. "Never."

He pats the top of the cab. "Go with God," he says, and salutes. "Tell Jorge Bush we're a kind people."

We catch the water truck quickly; still, we roll into Managua well before dark.

THE LIE

"Will I lose my eye?"
They do wonders with eyes these days.
You'll see.

"My hand – I play guitar."
They've got this great new technique
with tendons.

"Am I going to die?"
Not on my shift, you're not.
You're talking, that's a good sign.

"My son won't get here in time, will he?"
Take slow, deep breaths. I'll stay
until he gets here.

"Pray for me."
I'm praying for you
now.

Orientation 6.

Remember, all bleeding stops.

BACK HOME

We're strangers again, reflections withered.
Streaks of fine lightning scatter behind eyelids,
fireflies in fog, tracers in smoke.

Families, lovers mark this return from private stars,
remind our feet and our hands of articulation, our eyes
of visions, our mouths of a perfect language learned

one season too late, or too early. And so we
stumble back to this drizzle of confusion, this
trembling damp that we call *Love,* yes, and *Home.*

PICNIC IN LIMBO

Overcast skies in limbo. Sun a mere rumor
that poplars pass on. Jealous of light, draped in gray,
they wait. Fill this wait with green olives, cheese,
cold fried chicken. Clutch your basket
through those foggy hollows of twilight.

Your footprints stagger the sands ahead, amazed.
You sing to no one, no one applauds, pleased
at the gray, still gray. Even the ants don't show.

SCREAM

All dads don't scream in dreams, I know that now.
He did. I do, too, but less as time sorts out the
blare and glare. Always the wounded I left;
always their screams become my own.

Sharks stalked my dad, and the friendly fire, and
one kamikaze who slaughtered the ship's command.
Did he scream, too? Dad salvaged his belly flag—
a prayer to Emperor, to family, to a young, faceless love.

In the shriek and churn of battle, gagged by radio
silence, the shells that sank the *Atlanta* were his.
Shark-ripped sailors from both navies, young.
I sit up late with my coffee and cream, stave off dreams
with this notebook, my new pen, a blue vase of fresh red tulips.

AFTER THE WAR

Dad, when you start a war, can you quit anytime?
—Hali, age 7

A bloody dream dips and weaves
through damp, twisted sheets
and this deep night. Those dead
in our closet hunch at my feet,
whisper: *sleep tight   sleep tight*
 sleep   tight

EAVESDROPPING ON AMERICA

Women in the next booth compare shades of makeup,
shapes of their boyfriends' penises, prices of haircuts,
bikinis and blouses. They snap their gum, chainsmoke
and wonder how much their men love them—a dress,
trip to Hawaii, a new used car? Wars trouble them less
than reliability of the pill, pimples, their waiter's tight
black pants. They've had more men than years. With
army clothes and ignorance in fashion, Love takes its chances
here—a greenhorn smuggler sweating out roadblocks.
Outside, in the street, two rabbits nailed to a stop sign.
Where can Love, that thin guerrilla, take a stand?

INSTRUCTION FOR FEELING THE WAR

Turn up the heat in your bathroom. Higher.
Pour a bucket of dirt, clay and gravel into your tub,
mix well, add water to three fingers and stir.
Put on hiking clothes, pack everything you own
on your back, select a rifle that will save your life
and enough ammunition to hold off a SWAT team for a weekend.

Feel overloaded? Toss anything that's not food, rifle, ammunition.
Soak yourself with your garden hose and drag your pet
to the rooftop. Every gutter and vent is a trap. Leave
your pet. Hike back. Drop your rifle and your pack.
Eat four cold hot dogs and a jar of baby-food peaches.
Smoke whatever you have.

Keep those clothes and boots on; wrap yourself in the shower curtain
and curl up in the tub with your toilet paper in your pocket. Some kid
tosses fireworks in there a few times a night and turns the shower on.
If you want him to stop, you have to do this one more day.
Garnish the morning with bugs and serve over more cold hot dogs.
Don't change clothes, don't use the toilet; carry what you own off to work.

Shoot the first person you don't recognize; don't look at the eyes.
You can quit when someone who doesn't know what you're doing
says that you can stop. Take a shower. Pretend nothing happened.
Make love with your spouse, have a birthday with your children.
When they come for you, and they will come, don't fight back.
Tell them it's all okay, it's all cool; you had permission.

HOTEL OF LOST LIGHT

A low moan rises in the north, the lipless scream
of black wind whips these snags into masks of strangers.

We're all blown here when we slip our hold
and spin in one last long fall, brittle as death.

The old wolf slinks from hands and hair:
a private musk that wind and road and

wheezing rooms drive deep as childhood nightmare
into memory, gray, the only life we own.

FOOD CHAIN

Eisenhower shot Eddie Slovik for stealing bread,
For not killing Germans. After the forty days,
Christ ate what he could—stale bread, vinegar.
Gandhi stopped eating so his people wouldn't kill.

Somewhere a pride of hungry shadows scrapes stone, shifts weight.
Every border, every fence, bulkhead and screen, every curtain
strains to wall out hunger, wall in fine fat babies.
More ingenious than fruit, we fall any season.

Gandhi died with soup in his bowl, shot for rice,
his dead mouth gulping down the free sour wind.
We are the only netted fish who pull our own nets.
We are the only game we harvest we refuse to eat.

LIVING WILL

Burn me. Pay the fine, stand aside
and sift me through wind.

Wish I could see myself flake down over ferns,
moss, backs of beetles and crumbling stone.

I never looked better.

Remember my eyes to the sun.
My daughter, hold her tight as earth.

Look up these certain women. Be discreet
as the blush I never had. It's alright.

Their touch, like me, is gone.

A mouthful of ash and dust in the corners,
that's what I own. Peddle them if you can.

If you are my wife, sorry.
I hoard no secret wealth.

BREAKING DOWN

Slip the familiar action back; your room stuffs itself
with the quiet, wide-eyed stares of all your dead.
You didn't expect them. Lean your left temple
against the clean, hard bore. Feel your heartbeats

echo and re-echo down the chamber. This position
is uncomfortable. Remember the neighbor
years back whose brains and teeth filled the drapes
and chattered through your dreams forever? Slip

the safety off, breathe slow and sure as sleep. When
the car door slams in the driveway, and your wife
clatters up the steps, rush the rifle aside. Next morning,
feeding the chickens, notice the weeping salal and cedar.

You know it wasn't rain. You know, too, the long,
long time that they will spend in drying

REUNIÓN

Our hands forget the names of the dead
make promises we call love
unbutton, unhook, unzip winter.

This moan is the season
our tongues are tied to.

The afternoon drowses beside a gray stone.
Your scent, a lapful of petals.
Our bodies, a flutter of uncooped birds.

PROMISE

The drawer you keep
empty for my things.

DREAMING DAD

I'm hiding with a kid under a pile of stumps. Dead-
end alleyway, our burning breath. The patrol whispers
and *huffs* close, tobacco and gunpowder close, we
hold our breath, the kid and I, eye to eye so we don't
look at that boot punching through our tangle of roots.
A curse. He reaches to free himself, he sees....

Here I always gasp myself awake, pant good, clean
air, reassure my startled wife. But not tonight.

Tonight that boot crashes through the roots, a scapular
stuck on its laces, the picture a faded cameo of my dad.
I'm breathing slow now, deep, and the kid's gone. Patrol,
rubble, alley dissolve like snow in a glassblower's furnace.
Dad's full-size now, darkness behind him, shapeshifting
boxer, warrior, truck driver, cop. He smiles, wags
a thick finger. *Pay attention, Tiger. It's just a dream.*

Darkness swallows up his smile
and on the back of my breath he's gone.
                                    Tiger!

VETERAN RIDING FERRY

Half his face melts into his collar,
three fingers drip from his left cuff.

What passes for his right hand
scuttles the table for a smoke.
His skull tattoo warns us all,
"Airborne: Death From Above."

His pregnant wife swells her blouse,
their little girl strokes her dad's long hair.

One whole new face, all smiles behind him,
and already promise of another.

ABOUT THE AUTHOR

Bill Ransom was born in Puyallup, Washington, in 1945, and he began full-time employment at the age of eleven as an agricultural worker. He attended Washington State University on track and boxing scholarships, and the University of Puget Sound on a track scholarship. He received his BA in Sociology and English Education from the University of Washington in 1970.

From 1965 to 1970 Ransom worked as an expeditor on a quick engine change team, building and repairing military and commercial jet engines. He studied American Minority Literature and Old and Middle English on an NDEA Title IV Fellowship at the University of Nevada, Reno, then began a pilot project with the Poetry in the Schools program in Washington State. He received his MA in English from Utah State University. He founded and directed the popular Port Townsend Writers Conference for Centrum.

He was a firefighter, fire fighting basic training instructor, and CPR instructor for six years, and an advanced life support emergency medical technician for ten years in Jefferson County, Washington. He volunteers with humanitarian groups in Central America.

Ransom has published six novels, six poetry collections, numerous short stories and articles. Learning the Ropes (Utah State University Press), a collection of poetry, short fiction and essays, was billed as "a creative autobiography." Three of his short stories from this collection have been selections of the PEN/NEA syndicated fiction project, often called "the Pulitzer prize of the short story": "Uncle Hungry," "What Elena Said," and Learning the Ropes. These appeared in the Sunday Magazine editions of major newspapers around the country.

His poetry has been nominated for both the Pulitzer Prize and the National Book Award.

Bill Ransom currently serves as Academic Dean of Curriculum at the Evergreen State College in Olympia, Washington.

POET/TRANSLATORS

Zhang Er was born in Beijing, China and moved to New York City in 1986. Her poetry, non-fiction writing, and essays have appeared in publications in Taiwan, China, the American émigré community and in a number of American journals. She is the author of multiple books in Chinese and in English translation. She has read from her work at international festivals, conferences, reading series and universities in China, France, Portugal, Russia, Peru, Singapore, Hong Kong as well as in the U.S. She currently teaches at Evergreen-Tacoma.

Lü De'an, a native of Fujian province, was born in 1960. His initial interest in poetry was sparked by the emergence of the so-called "obscure" poets at the end of the 1970s, and his friendship with Shu Ting, another Fukienese who is probably one of the most extraordinary Chinese poets of the second half of the twentieth century, but he trained as a commercial artist, and has learned much from modernist painting as a poet. He was associated with the Nanjing-based 'Them' [Tamen] group, and published frequently in its unofficial journal which was launched in 1985.

Ying Qin was born in 1975 in Shandong Province, P. R. China. She obtained a Master's degree in Chemistry from Fudan University in Shanghai in 1997. She worked as an editor at Shanghai Far-East Publishing House for a year, then came to the United States to study at University of Rhode Island. She holds two Master's degrees, one in Computer Science (2002) and another in English Literature (2005). She's currently in the Ph.D. program in the Department of East Asian Languages and Literature at U. Wisconsin Madison, studying classical Chinese literature.

ABOUT THE ARTIST

Joe Feddersen was born in Omak, Washington, in 1953, of Okanagan and Lakes heritage. He spent his childhood roaming the basins and rolling hills of Omak and the Colville Indian Reservation. Joe Feddersen earned his BFA degree at the University of Washington and his MFA degree at the University of Wisconsin, studying with such legendary printmakers as Glen Alps in Seattle and Dean Meeker in Madison. A faculty member at the Evergreen State College since the late 1980s, Feddersen has emerged as one of the foremost Native American artists of our region.

Joe Feddersen: Vital Signs, a retrospective of his work, has been published by the University of Washington Press. His work explores the interrelationships between urban place markers and indigenous landscapes.